*"Never in the field of human conflict
was so much owed by so many
to so few. . . ."*

The Battle of Britain marks a decisive moment in history, a crucial turning point in the course of World War II for England and America. In the golden weeks of late summer, 1940, the exhausted young pilots of the RAF rose to meet the fury of the Luftwaffe—the most powerful and destructive air force yet built—and beat back Goering's flyers to save England from invasion and defeat.

Now those dramatic weeks are once again brought to life in a spectacular, vividly authentic film. In this fascinating in-depth story of the greatest war film ever made, Book-of-the-Month author Leonard Mosley tells how a seemingly impossible project developed over four years into a $20,000,000 motion picture involving Sir Laurence Olivier, Adolf Galland, Susannah York, Sir Michael Redgrave, Michael Caine, a skyful of Spitfires and German 109's gathered from the four corners of the world, and a vast team of technicians, cameramen, and RAF experts in a stunning reconstruction of the historic air battle that saved Britain in World War II.

BATTLE OF BRITAIN

A HARRY SALTZMAN PRODUCTION

starring

Senior Civil Servant	HARRY ANDREWS
Sqn. Ldr. Canfield	MICHAEL CAINE
Air Vice Marshal Keith Park	
Air Officer Commanding No. 11 Group	TREVOR HOWARD
Baron Von Richter	CURT JURGENS
Sgt. Pilot Andy	IAN McSHANE
Group Captain Baker	KENNETH MORE
Air Chief Marshal Sir Hugh Dowding	
Air Officer Commanding-in-Chief	
Fighter Command	LAURENCE OLIVIER
Group Captain Hope	NIGEL PATRICK
Flt. Lt.-Sqn. Ldr. Harvey	CHRISTOPHER PLUMMER
Air Vice Marshall Evill	MICHAEL REDGRAVE
British Minister in Switzerland	RALPH RICHARDSON
Sqn. Ldr. Skipper	ROBERT SHAW
Air Vice Marshal Trafford Leigh-Mallory	
Air Officer Commanding No. 12 Group	
	PATRICK WYMARK
Section Officer Maggie Harvey	SUSANNAH YORK

technical credits

Produced by Harry Saltzman and S. Benjamin Fisz
Directed by Guy Hamilton
Screenplay by James Kennaway and Wilfred Greatorex
Color by Technicolor—Filmed in Panavision
Director of Photography—Freddie Young B.S.C.

British Technical and Tactical Advisors:
>   Group Captain Hamish Mahaddie, Group Captain Tom Gleave, Wing Commander Robert Stanford Tuck, Squadron Leader Ginger Lacey, Squadron Leader B. Drobinski, Squadron Leader Robert Wright, Wing Commander Claire Legge (W.R.A.F.)

German Technical and Tactical Advisors:
>   Lt. General Adolf Galland, Colonel Hans Brustellin, Major Franz Frodl

the Battle of Britain
the making of a film

Leonard Mosley

BALLANTINE BOOKS • NEW YORK

BALLANTINE BOOKS, INC.
101 Fifth Avenue, New York, N.Y. 10003

Contents

As It Was in 1940

No one is prepared to state with any certainty exactly when the Battle of Britain began. Most English historians choose July 10, 1940, for it was on that day that Me-109 fighters and Stuka dive-bombers of the German Luftwaffe first came swarming across the English Channel in force. They had been ordered to close that narrow waterway to British shipping by sinking everything they found afloat. Hurricanes roared out to meet them and there were dogfights throughout the day. Thirteen German planes were shot down and the RAF lost six Hurricanes.

On the other hand, the Germans (those, that is, who are prepared to admit that there was any such event as the Battle of Britain) choose August 13, 1940. It is marked as Adlertag, or Eagle's Day, in German records. On that drizzly, cloudy summer's day the Luftwaffe flew 1,485 fighter and bomber sorties against targets in England, mostly against RAF airfields. The RAF shot down forty-five Nazi bombers and fighters for a loss of thirteen of their own, but several of their fields were put out of action.*

* All figures quoted come from postwar records taken from both RAF and Luftwaffe documents.

1

Thereafter the attacks intensified and the Battle of Britain was well and truly joined. The fate of these islands and the outcome of the war depended upon the bravery of the pilots who fought it and the skill of their superiors on the ground who gave them their orders.

Since the end of June, the German armies had been masters of Western Europe. France had capitulated and signed an armistice with Adolf Hitler. Britain's Army had retreated by way of Dunkirk, limping back across the Channel to England minus most of its weapons. Now the fighters and bombers of the German Luftwaffe were moving in. They had already established bases in Occupied Norway, from which they could attack Scotland and the Royal Navy base at Scapa Flow; and with the capture of Holland, Belgium, and France, they began bringing in the fighters and the bombers which would pound England finally into defeat. From their nearest bases in France, German fighters were only four minutes' flight away from Dover harbour.

Adolf Hitler made plenty of mistakes in World War II, but perhaps his most serious was his failure to attack England in force and invade her shores immediately after the collapse of France. There was plenty of brave talk of fighting in the streets and on the beaches, and there is no doubt that Britons would have fought and died bravely to defend their shores against the Nazi invader. It is doubtful, however, whether they could have kept him out at that time. Weapons were desperately short. The troops who had retreated from Dunkirk were exhausted and low in spirits. Scores of planes had been lost trying to stem the German advance across the Low Countries and France, and the RAF was desperately short of planes

2

and pilots. Their position would have been worse had not Sir Hugh Dowding, head of Fighter Command, fought Churchill and the Cabinet and reluctantly persuaded them not to send any more fighters to France. Otherwise he would have had no aircraft at all to meet the Germans when they came.

Why did they not come?

One of these days, when the official documents are released, the full story will be told of an elaborate game of bluff which Churchill and his diplomats played in this critical moment in Britain's history.

Adolf Hitler could not believe that the British would fight on alone after the collapse of France. How could they possibly survive the onslaught of his air force and his armies—which had already smashed Poland and humiliated France? They were bound to sue for peace. And if they did so (he told his friend, Mussolini, the Italian dictator) he would be magnanimous with them.

So in every neutral capital where there were British and German diplomatic representatives, word was spread that the Germans were ready to talk. The British (without ever saying so officially) in turn indicated that they were not unwilling to discuss possible terms. In fact, they were bluffing. Though there may have been some elements willing to talk peace with the Nazis in 1940, Churchill was not one of them. He was, in fact, bluffing—and playing for time. Time to re-equip the Army and rebuild its morale. Time, above all, to repair the gaps in the air defenses of Britain in the readiness for the moment when Hitler realized that the enemy would not capitulate and must be forced to her knees.

In this way, Britain won six or seven of the most valuable weeks in her history. The German armies waited. Save for sporadic sorties over southern England and Scotland, the Luftwaffe stayed on the ground. And in the factories where the Hurricanes and Spitfires of the RAF were being made, work went on around the clock to build new fighters and send them out to the waiting squadrons.

By July 10, 1940, it was evident that Hitler at long last suspected that the British had been fooling him. That day he gave the commander of his air forces, Reichsmarschall Herman Göring, permission to close the English Channel by sinking all ships sailing on it and smashing all south coast harbors from Dover to Southampton. The British realized that the time had come at last, that their bluff had been called. Reconnaissance and intelligence reports confirmed that hundreds of German invasion barges were moving through the canals towards the Channel coast.

It was just about this time that Hitler made his most overt attempt to bring the British to the peace table. He used as his intermediary King Gustav of Sweden, who indicated that the Germans were ready to make proposals, but also that they wanted an unequivocal answer.

Churchill gave it in a statement which said, in part:

"Before any such requests or proposals could even be considered it would be necessary that effective guarantees by deeds, not words, should be forthcoming from Germany which would ensure the restoration of the free and independent life of Czechoslovakia, Poland, Norway, Denmark, Holland, Belgium and, above all, France."

Hitler was amazed. But if that was the way the British wanted it—to be crushed by sheer force—then that was the way it would be. He issued a directive to his armed forces outlining his plan for Operation

4

Seelöwe (Sea lion), the invasion of Britain. But first he called in Reichsmarschall Göring and told him to clear the way by wiping out the Royal Air Force.

"We will be in control of the skies in a matter of days, mein führer," the fat Luftwaffe leader replied.

Thanks to the young pilots of the RAF—and thanks to some tactical errors on the part of the Luftwaffe—he was wrong.

But only just. . . .

Prologue "Heinkel Leader-Turn Left, Left For Duxford!"

———◆———

THE CLOUDS HUNG low over the flat farmlands of East Anglia on the afternoon of May 14, 1968. A brisk and unseasonably chill wind whipped in from the North Sea and flattened the grass alongside the runways of Duxford airfield. In the squat control tower on the edge of the field a group of men sat around a trestle table; they listened with half an ear to the chatter of faint voices and the crackle of static from a radio transmitter in front of them. One of them, a dapper, pink-faced man with a bristled ginger moustache, stared gloomily over the airfield toward the curdling clouds on the gray horizon and shook his head.

"It's no day for welcoming foreign visitors," he said in a flat Lancashire voice.

"Not in the crates *they're* flying, it isn't!" said the RAF warrant officer standing beside him.

The telephone rang and the man with the bristle moustache picked it up. "Chadwick here! Yes, they're on their way—south of the Thames at the moment.

What's that? The weather? Bloody awful! But don't worry. We'll get them down."

He put down the telephone and resumed his gloomy stare across the field. The voices over the radio transmitter were getting louder and clearer now. It began to be apparent that some of the chatter was in Spanish.

An RAF air commodore came into the tower, a row of war medals spread across his chest.

"Things don't improve, do they?" he said in a jaunty voice. "Take the weather, for instance. Now when I was at Duxford in 1940, they always laid on sunshine for us. . . ."

Duxford airfield. It lies beside the main road that leads to Cambridge and Newmarket, two English towns both famous, the first for its university, the second for its racecourse and its bloodstock. But in 1940 Duxford superseded both in importance, for here was one of the nerve centers of a battle that changed the course and the nature of World War II. That summer France had been defeated and overrun by the victorious armies of the German Reich. Britain had left much of her army and most of her equipment on the other side of the English Channel on the beaches of Dunkirk. Hitler had announced his ultimatum: Britain must sue for surrender or his air force (his invincible Luftwaffe) would smash her.

So when Britain refused to surrender, the planes came over from bases as far apart as Norway and France. Those in France were only ten minutes away from British soil and only forty minutes from London. It was from Duxford and other bases that the Spitfire and Hurricane fighters of the Royal Air Force roared off to meet the Messerschmitts and Heinkels sent to pound England into defeat. The dog-fights which these planes fought in the skies over the Thames estuary, the Kent fruit fields and the English Channel are now known to the world as the Battle of Britain.

Now, on this stormy May afternoon twenty-eight years later, the Messerschmitts were on their way again; and once more there would be a Spitfire and a Hurricane in the sky, waiting for them. But not to do battle this time, not for the moment, anyway.

The Messerschmitts, seventeen of them, and two Heinkel 11 bombers, had left southern Spain five days earlier to fly across Europe to England. (Why they were in Spain in the first place will emerge later in this story, as will the reason why most of their pilots were Spanish.) It had been a hazardous journey all the way. For one thing, the weather had been against them, and the elements, as if infuriated at seeing Nazi planes with swastikas on their tails once more riding the skies, had flung every cosmic obstacle in their way from fog and thunderstorms to torrential hail and rain. Then there had been the physical risk of subjecting such ancient flying monuments of World War II to the strains of a transcontinental journey of such length; for though accompanying planes carried cargoes of spare parts, what if metal fatigue caused a crack-up over the Pyrenees or the peaks of the Massif Central? And perhaps most difficult of all, there had been the tricky diplomatic job of persuading the authorities in Paris to allow planes wearing the swastika to land in France, where they had once been the hated symbols of defeat and occupation.

But now they were on the last lap, with only two temporary casualties—a Messerschmitt and a Heinkel —stranded en route. This morning of May 14 they had come in ("downsun" in the true fighter fashion) from the English Channel and swooped across the white

cliffs of Dover, as they had done so much more arrogantly and malevolently in 1940, and then they had
wheeled north toward the Thames estuary and their
new home fifty miles beyond it, at Duxford.

There we waited for them: a delegation of brass
hats from the Royal Air Force, an eager group of
press photographers and reporters, a Spitfire and a
Hurricane in the sky above. And a film company
which would be taking over the planes from now on.

"Spitfire red leader, can you hear me?"

Chadwick had given up fingering his bristle moustache and contemplating the weather and now had
earphones over his head and a microphone in his
hand. Above us, somewhere in the clouds, we could
hear the baritone throb of Merlin engines as the Spitfire and the Hurricane circled in readiness for the
rendezvous.

"We are expecting our foreign visitors in ten minutes, Spitfire red leader," Chadwick said. "Keep your
eye open for them."

The jabber of Spanish over the transmitter was
very loud now, but suddenly a louder and very English voice broke in:

"Spitfire red leader here. I have sighted our visitors." His level tone suddenly took on a note of excitement. "They're quite a sight, aren't they?" And then
to his comrade in the Hurricane: "You ready, Joe?
Remember, they don't know we're here. Let's go in
and surprise them!"

We could hear the rising note of the engines as
they peeled off and started their dive through the
clouds.

Riding hard on the incoming Messerschmitts that
afternoon was a remarkable character named Coman-
dante Pedro de Santa Cruz. Santa Cruz has been

flying fighter aircraft in combat ever since the Spanish civil war; he commanded a Spanish fighter squadron flying with the Germans on the Russian front in World War II; he is tough, skillful and nerveless. But even his Me-109 faltered in its flight and started to take evasive action as the Spitfire and the Hurricane zoomed in across his flight path and then wiggled their wings in a greeting.

As for the Heinkel at the head of the formation which was supposed to lead the planes on to the approach run for Duxford . . .

Through a window of the control tower down on the ground the face of an excited RAF corporal appeared.

"Aircraft in sight at the end of the airfield!" he shouted.

Chadwick nodded. He spoke urgently into his microphone:

"Heinkel leader, Heinkel leader. This is Duxford. If you read me, turn left. The airfield is on your left!"

A splutter of anguished Spanish over the intercom. A Spanish-speaking RAF lieutenant sitting beside Chadwick listened intently and then said:

"He says okay. He's got you. The airfield is on his right."

Chadwick: "Not right. Left! Hallo, Heinkel leader. Turn left a hundred and eighty degrees. The airfield is on your left."

A magpie chatter of Spanish. The Spanish-speaking RAF type:

"It's all right. He understands. He's turning a hundred and eighty degrees right."

The anguished face of the RAF corporal through the window:

"Sir, they've gone. Buggered off, the lot of them!"

There followed a heavy thirty seconds of silence broken only by crackling static, and then suddenly a crisp voice came on to the intercom.

"Hallo, Duxford. This is RAF ground control, Coltishall. Are you looking for a bunch of Messerschmitt fighters and a Heinkel bomber, by any chance? They've just passed over us and, as far as I can see from my radar, they are now making a rather low circular tour of Cambridge University. Don't you think you'd better call them back—and do the tour by bus instead?"

But half an hour later they were dropping down through the wind and mist onto the runways of Duxford. First Santa Cruz turned at the end of the field, yawing slightly as the stiff crosswind caught him, and then trimmed his craft and touched down for a perfect three-point landing. Other, clumsier landings followed. One pilot, short of fuel, his batteries flat and his radio gone, practically sliced the roof off the control tower as he tried to discover whether his landing wheels were down. They gave him the green Very light and he came in. One by one, the others followed. The pilots lined up to be greeted by the visiting RAF brass hats while the Spitfire and the Hurricane did a low level beat-up over their heads by way of a final salute.

Then everyone made their way to the newly built mess across the road, and there, that night, much Spanish wine and brandy was drunk, many impassioned speeches were made, and the Spanish waiters openly wept as toasts were drunk to Anglo-Spanish friendship.

Out on Duxford airfield, the Messerschmitts were lined up, their engine cowls carefully battened down to protect them from the rigors of their first summer on English soil. An old airman walked past them in the gathering twilight and clicked his lips as he stared at the Nazi swastikas on the tail of each plane.

"Well now," he said. "It's a strange sight, isn't it? Considering the fact that we won the war, I never thought I'd ever see a squadron of those buggers sitting on our airfields."

There was distaste on his face as he looked at them.

It was an expression that was to change to a kind of affection before very long. For those seventeen Messerschmitts were in for a hard, rough summer, compared with which their flight across Europe and their arrival at Duxford would be looked back on as a joyride.

The filming of the flying sequences for a production called *The Battle of Britain* was about to begin, and soon these single-engined fighters would be diving, banking, rolling and looping through the English skies at the same speed and with the same intensive skill as they had once done in 1940.

Only this was 1968, and there were crises ahead.

I

Birth Pangs of an Epic

———◆———

THERE HAVE BEEN over 150 books written about the Battle of Britain by authors of such diverse nationalities as American, Australian, British, Czech, French, German, New Zealand, Polish and South African. Most of them have sold well. Some have been best sellers in every country in the world. It therefore seems strange that no one—either in Britain or in Hollywood—had attempted until 1968 to transfer the subject to the cinema screen. True, there have been films (such as *Angels One Five* and *Reach for the Sky*) which dealt with some phases of the battle as they impinged upon a particular flying unit or personality; but none which tried to convey, in addition, the overall nature of the battle and the tremendous issues involved.

Yet the Battle of Britain has all the elements of great drama: shape particularly, for it all took place in one short English summer; a great and easily comprehensible issue, for if Britain won the battle she survived, if Germany won it she had won the war; the clash of personalities on the ground between British and German commanders struggling not only to outsmart each other but to fight off the intriguers inside

13

their own camps; and the young men in their machines up in the air, the heroic pawns in the great game.

It may well be that the epic cinematic story of the Battle of Britain has had to wait twenty-eight years to be made because only now can the whole truth be shown on the screen. New facts have begun to emerge from hitherto unpublishable documents which tend to show that the battle was not quite as black-and-white as it has hitherto seemed, that it was not just a clash between the heroic English and the villainous Huns, but that there were "goodies" and "baddies" on both sides. To make a film of the Battle of Britain which sees the encounter whole instead of from one often biased point of view, it is necessary to portray some events which have hitherto been too unpalatable for either the British or the Germans to swallow: not least, that there were real villains and real cowards as well as real heroes in both camps.

So perhaps the film had to wait for the world to digest the slanted, emotional, sentimentalized view of the Battle of Britain before attempting to face the harsher but much more exciting truth. If so, one would be tempted to praise a man named S. Benjamin Fisz for having been inspired to choose just the right moment for launching the project. It is tempting but it isn't quite true. Like many another event of some moment, the film of *The Battle of Britain* happened almost fortuitously.

Ben Fisz has been connected with British films since 1945, when he was demobilized from the Polish air force (for which he flew as a Hurricane pilot in World War II). He has since become sufficiently well known in the film world to be called Ben or Benny without anyone needing further identification. He is a large, pale, fleshy man very conscious of his tendency

to run to corpulence and always on the verge of starting or finishing a new diet, in spite of which he con-
tinues, like the late Dylan Thomas, to look like an
unmade bed. Though he is a keen reader of English
literature and poetry (Thomas included), he speaks the
language in a sort of Mittel European telegraphese
which make him as oft-quoted at Pinewood or Elstree
as Goldwyn used to be in Hollywood.

In September 1965, Fisz had just completed the
production of a film called *The Heroes of Telemark,*
a story of Norwegian resistance fighters in German-
occupied Norway, which had been directed by his
friend Anthony Mann. For Fisz it was the biggest film
he had made so far, and potentially the most rewarding; it had received good notices from the British and
European critics, it had pleased the heads of the
Rank Film Organization, which had put up money to
finance it; and he was eager to exploit his standing by
setting up his next film as soon as possible. He already had a subject and a well-cherished one: he
wished to make a film about the late Major General
Orde Wingate, a non-Jewish Zionist mystic who, in
the course of his career in the British army, managed
at the same time to organize the Israeli (Haganah)
guerrillas in British-occupied Palestine, and later
ousted the Italians and put Emperor Haile Selassie
back on the throne of Ethiopia. Fisz held the rights to
the two major books on the subject; all he needed
was the consent of Wingate's relatives to allow him to
go forward with the project, which Rank in England
and Twentieth Century Fox in the U.S. would spon-
sor. The family consent was expected and what he
awaited was the actual signature on the legal document. On the morning of September 13, 1965, the
telephone rang in his small Mayfair office just off Park

Lane. The relatives had changed their minds and would no longer sign a consent.

"It was like punch in solar plexus," said Fisz in his telegraphese. "I was personally surprised. I walked out of my office with pain in head not knowing what to do."

Luckily for him, his office is only a few yards from the green fields of Hyde Park and there for some time he paced the grass, rocking his head to ease his distress; the receipts from *Telemark* had not yet begun to come in, and his situation would be dire, as well as his credit, if he could not set up another deal as quickly as possible.

It was then that he heard the drone of engines flying overhead—piston engines, not jets—and looked up at a sound which was only too familiar. A Spitfire and a Hurricane fighter were flying over the park. He noticed that other people were looking up too, and that the younger ones among them were puzzled. "What kind of planes are those?" they were asking. (In fact, the two fighters were going through a rehearsal of the flypast over London two days later in honor of the official Battle of Britain Day, September 15.)

Fisz hurried back to his office and telephoned his friend Freddy Thomas, head of the production division of the Rank Organization.

"Freddy, dear friend," he said, "did you like film of *Longest Day?*"

"It made us a lot of money," Thomas replied cautiously.*

Fisz: "How about film about Battle of Britain done same way? You know, both sides given fair play in story."

Thomas (after a pause): "It would depend on what the script was like."

---

* The Rank Organization's chain of theaters showed it in England and distributed it in the Eastern Hemisphere.

Fisz: "Don't worry. That's the big surprise. You'll be delighted with the writer I have in mind."

Thomas: "In that case, you'd better come and see me."

There is a belligerent streak in Benny Fisz. He once broke the nose of a fellow Polish pilot who called him a "Jewish trickster" after a card game, and one of the stars of *The Battle of Britain* still does not know how closely he came to getting the same treatment when he made a slighting reference to Fisz's background during the making of the film. But his principal quality is charm, ingratiating and persuasive charm, and when he exerts it to the full there are few men or women who can resist it. By the time he had completed the telephone conversation with Thomas, Fisz's own imagination had caught fire and he realized the possibilities of the project he had so inadventently snatched from the air. In the next few days he put his charm to work wherever it was most likely to do good, and came back with results. He lunched with the playwright Terence Rattigan, and they strolled out of the restaurant happily arm in arm at the end of it. He dined with old acquaintances at the Air Ministry, and left ripples of enthusiasm lapping around the air commodores.

It was at this point that he made a discovery which seemed likely to consolidate the Rank Organization's interest in the film. He pointed out that they owned the film rights of one of the books dealing with the Battle of Britain, *The Thin Blue Line* by Charles Graves. Thereafter, whenever the Rank Organization wrote to him they referred to the project as *The Battle of Britain (The Thin Blue Line)* or even, on certain occasions, as *The Thin Blue Line (The Battle of Britain)*.

Still, in the short run it was useful, for it gave

Freddy Thomas a trump card to put before his board of directors, particularly his formidable chairman, John Davis, in his determination to "sell" the film to them. By mid-October 1965, such progress had been made in their joint discussions that Fisz was able to write to Thomas on October 15:

Dear Freddy,

BATTLE OF BRITAIN

A few notes to keep you au courant with our plans for the above. The Air Ministry will cooperate and will provide us with nine Spitfires. They will also provide a number of German aircraft up to the amount we will need, and will put pilots and crew at our disposal to fly them.* They will also put Duxford airfield at our disposal, as this airfield has not been changed since the war. Lewis Gilbert is anxious to direct the picture and Terence Rattigan has agreed to write a draft script for the ridiculous amount of $8,000. It is planned to shoot the picture at Pinewood and have it ready for the Battle of Britain anniversary on September 15, 1967.

The idea is to make the picture on the line of *The Longest Day*, that is to see both sides of the story, as the younger generation has no idea of what it was all about. All the German parts will be played by Germans with subtitles.

Casting possibilities: Jimmy Fox, young pilot officer; Michael Caine, sergeant pilot; Tom Courtenay; Susannah York or Sarah Miles. Older types like Peter Finch, Stanley Baker, Peter O'Toole, Kenneth More, and special roles for Mason, Guinness, Richardson, Redgrave, Olivier. Special effects: Robert Fulton; camera: either Freddy Young or Robert Krasker.

This will be the biggest picture ever made in Great Britain, and possibly the biggest in the world.

Sincerely,

Ben

---

* This suggestion that the Air Ministry would provide all the planes needed for the film was wildly optimistic, as it turned out.

By this time Fisz was feeling on top of the world, convinced that the cameras would soon be turning on the film of *The Battle of Britain*. So far, nothing had been signed. A request he had made to Freddy Thomas that Rank advance him $14,000 "to cover expenses of various kinds" was ignored, but he did not let this cast him down. Instead he flew to Hollywood for conferences with Terence Rattigan about the script, and there he ran into his first setback. Rattigan was working at that time on the script of a black comedy about the Black Hole of Calcutta called *The Nine Tiger Man*, and it soon became apparent that he would not be able to finish it in time to produce a draft script of *The Battle of Britain* for March 1966, which is the date Fisz had given Rank. In any case, Rattigan's New York agent had hit the ceiling when he learned of the terms his client had verbally agreed to with his friend Fisz. (The deal they had tentatively talked about was one whereby Rattigan received $8,000 for preparing a draft script against $100,000 for the complete shooting script.) His agent pointed out that the price for a Rattigan script was 100,000 pounds not dollars ($280,000 at the then rate of exchange) and he would not hear of him accepting less, "not even for the Union Jack."

Whether any news of this development reached the Rank Organization is not certain, but early in December 1965, Fisz found a letter waiting for him from Freddy Thomas in which *The Thin Blue Line* was pointedly mentioned and then the words:

"I propose that for these early stages we treat the film as a Rank Film Production and when we get to the appropriate stage everything could be assigned to the appropriate production company."

There was also a note to say that a check for $1,400

was on its way to him "to be accounted for by you" against a further $4,200, and "we will then take stock of the situation prevailing."

To Fisz this meant only one thing. Rank were trying to steal his baby! He wrote back:

"Your letter of December 6 astonished me. In the first place, my original idea was *The Battle of Britain* and it was I who called attention to the fact that the Rank Organization owned one of the many stories on the subject. I brought the idea to you because I thought my project might be of interest to you because of your ownership of this work." He went on to repeat that *The Thin Blue Line* was but one of the works dealing with the Battle of Britain and that it was his firm intention to have a completely original script for the film. And then he reached the main point of his letter: "You are trying to take over my project. At the risk of parting company with you on this project, I refuse to be treated as a B-picture producer.

To which Thomas coolly replied:

Dear Ben, *The Thin Blue Line* (*Battle of Britain*)

I am equally surprised to get your letter of December 8 in reply to mine of December 6. Let me first at least clarify one point. We are not as you seem to think trying to take over your project. My letter of November 17 surely makes it clear that at an appropriate stage we would assign the rights to the appropriate production company. Until that point has been reached, it is not unreasonable when big money is being paid out for Rank to have security, and the only security at this point would be to have the rights of the script. . . .

Thomas did not go on to labor the point, but it was clear that until there was a script there would be no deal, and in the meantime Rank was cherishing *The Thin Blue Line* to its bosom and thinking of the whole project as a Rank, rather than a Ben Fisz, film production.

Fisz is nothing if not an optimist (*The Battle of Britain* would never have been made had he not been), and he continued his preparations for the film as if everything had been signed and sealed. A new scriptwriter (James Kennaway) was engaged in place of Rattigan; Fisz appointed an agent whose job it would henceforth be to track down World War II fighters and bombers in whatever country they might be lying; he held repeated conferences at the Air Ministry in search of cooperation once filming started. But even as late as the spring of 1966, when the film would have to start to be ready for 1967, nothing had been signed by the Rank Organization. There was, in fact, a hiatus in the negotiations which Fisz did not seem to recognize and the Rank Organization would have been unwilling to admit, but which was nonetheless real. It was not, in fact, until May 1966 that something happened to break the unadmitted deadlock. Early that month (the date has been difficult to pin down) the telephone rang in Fisz's office and a voice said:

"Benny? This is Harry. Look, how about having dinner with me tonight at the White Tower?"

It was the voice of Harry Saltzman. He was about to come into the film, and things would begin to move again.

It would be difficult to imagine two characters more different in temperament and outlook than Ben Fisz and Harry Saltzman, even though both are Jewish. They are, in fact, prime examples of the influence and importance of environment. Ben Fisz, born and brought up in the anti-Semitic atmosphere of prewar

Poland, only a couple of generations from the ghetto, weaned on fearsome stories of bloody Polish and Russian pogroms, comes from a background where a Jew who raised his voice and demanded his rights was lucky to get away with a flogging with the knout. He learned by instinct that the way to get what he wanted was by patience, blandness—charm, of course, too—but above all, patience.

Any ghettolike grit in the mind of Harry Saltzman was blown away by the breezes from Lake Erie which swept across Cleveland, Ohio, where he spent his boyhood. Right from the start he was always prepared to fight for what he wanted, and right from the start he was restless. He ran away from home at the age of sixteen to join a traveling circus and a year later he was traveling with it through France and Spain. It was the beginning of a gypsy life which hasn't ended yet, even though he has now planted his roots in England. Those were the years of intensive self-education. The fluent French and rough Spanish and German he speaks today were picked up from the stagehands, the roustabouts and the double-acts for whom he worked in the traveling rings and the small provincial variety theaters of Europe. In 1937 he helped to get a whole circus out of Barcelona, an hour or two ahead of Franco's armies during the civil war, by putting them to sea in a leaky boat and all but thumbing a lift from passing liners. In 1940, at the time the Battle of Britain was being fought over the English Channel, Saltzman was in Hollywood working on his first film as assistant director to René Clair.

He came to England after war service in France with the Canadian air force and the U.S. Office of War Information, but left again to make TV films in Italy and Spain. But he came back again in the 1950s and was quick to smell the atmosphere of change and social discontent in England at the time. The rebellion was beginning against the class barriers, the Establishment, the bourgeois values of the prewar years, and his ear caught the murmurs against tradition and accepted values by the young and the upcoming. He spent much time at the new and experimental theater in Sloane Square, the Royal Court, and became an admirer of its director-in-chief, George Devine, and a friend of two of its brashest and brightest members, an actor-playwright named John Osborne and a director, Tony Richardson. With the last two he combined to form Woodfall Films to bring the first of the so-called "kitchen sink" dramas to the screen. It was Osborne's *Look Back in Anger* with Richard Burton and Mary Ure, and it was followed by another film adaptation of an Osborne play, *The Entertainer*, with Laurence Olivier. But it was the third film which Saltzman masterminded for Woodfall, *Saturday Night and Sunday Morning*, with Albert Finney and rough sexual goings-on among the proletariat, which brought about a real revolution in British films. For the first time the hero came from the working class and spoke with a provincial accent but was no figure of fun, as anyone who dropped his aitches usually had been before this film. The cinema-going masses (particularly the women) took the new kind of hero to their bosom, and Woodfall was suddenly in the money.

It was inevitable that a dominating character like Saltzman and two temperamental artists of the caliber of Osborne and Richardson must clash. Saltzman is no man for running a business by committee or majority vote, and a split was unavoidable. In any case, he saw an end to the craze for "kitchen sink" and realized, as conditions improved in England, that the country, and possibly the world, was beginning to search instead for escape from domestic problems. They wanted fun—and fantasy. It was then that he joined forces with a fellow American based in London, Cubby Broccoli, to buy the rights of Ian Fleming's spy stories and start the craze for the never-never world of James Bond.

When they met for dinner at the White Tower restaurant in Soho in May 1966, Ben Fisz must have guessed what Harry Saltzman wanted of him. The Bond films would go on, like a Tarzan series of the sixties, for as long as he wanted to make them, but the zest he once had in masterminding them had obviously dissipated. Fisz knew Saltzman's way of thinking well enough to understand how much the idea of *The Battle of Britain* must appeal to him. The time was ripe for a different kind of war epic, one which told the truth about war but one which, by its very nature, couldn't help being dramatically spectacular at the same time. It brought together the two sides in Saltzman's nature—his passion for history and the Reason Why and his unquenchable sense of showmanship.

Fisz must have guessed, too, what Saltzman's advent would mean. *The Battle of Britain* would no longer be his exclusive baby. With Saltzman as a partner, a dominating father would have come on the scene.

On the other hand, what choice had he? Harry Saltzman was a power in the film world and when he embarked on a project, studios listened with attention and banks reached for their check books. Could the film get off the ground without him?

"I would like to come into *The Battle of Britain*," Saltzman said that evening. "The subject interests me. What is the situation?"

Fisz: "Rank is prepared to put up part of the

money in return for a percentage of world profits and the Eastern Hemisphere rights."

Saltzman: "How much will they put up?"

Fisz: "Four million, two hundred thousand dollars." *

Saltzman: "How much do you visualize your budget?"

Fisz: "Eight to ten million."

Saltzman: "I can get the rest."

"When you go into a deal," says Ben Fisz, "it is like a marriage, you make it for good or for worse."

In the next few weeks there were plenty of trials and tribulations to test out the new relationship. At first all went smoothly. The advent of Saltzman into the film galvanized the Rank Organization, and within a week or two Freddy Thomas was writing to "Harry and Ben" to confirm that his studios would participate in the production and "will put out by way of guarantee a maximum of $3,500,000" in return for 20 percent of the world profits and the rights to the Eastern Hemisphere distribution of the film. They would also put up $140,000 as preproduction money for expenses. But Thomas added that all this was contingent on Rank's approval of the final script and the budget. He added:

"We note that it will now be a Harry Saltzman presentation and not a joint presentation."

To Saltzman it was obvious that the most urgent priority now was to see a finished script of the film. Rank needed it before they would risk their money; he did not agree that they should approve it, for he had already decided that only he, Fisz and the director should have final approval of how *The Battle of Britain*

---

* It was, in fact, $3,500,000.

should be screened, but he did need something to show them in return for their money.

But that was the trouble. For the moment there was no finished script, and it didn't look as if there would be one for some time to come. James Kennaway had been working on it for some time now, with Ben Fisz breathing heavily over his shoulder. By this time Fisz knew exactly what he wanted to see in the screenplay. He had always been knowledgeable about the Battle of Britain and since the idea of the film first came to him he had done his homework.

"The result was," he said, "that I was at least a hundred and fifty books ahead of anybody else on the subject. James had to bone up on the battle too, and that took time. To get what I wanted into the script he had to study the new research. I sent him to Germany to talk to ex-pilots over there. But it took time, time, time. James was under very heavy pressure."

It was at this moment that Saltzman brought Guy Hamilton into the film. He had recently finished shooting *Funeral in Berlin* with Michael Caine for Saltzman, who was pleased with the final result. He took Hamilton out to lunch.

"*Funeral's* so good," he said, "I'm going to give you a present."

"How much?" asked Hamilton.

"Not how much—how wonderful! I'm going to let you direct *The Battle of Britain*. You're just the man I'm looking for," said Saltzman, happily.

Ben Fisz was not so enchanted. "I personally didn't like the idea of Guy at first. I knew him very well and his films: *Touch of Larceny, Manuela, The Best of Enemies*. Good but too light for what *Battle* needed, I thought. But then I got a beautiful surprise. After

26

many meetings I could see that Guy was hooked on story. He saw he could do something with it—make it tough, uncompromising, true but dramatic and startling."

This, however, also took up time while Hamilton read the books and the research, while he too talked to British and German ex-pilots, while he too got involved. After which there were endless conferences with Kennaway while the drives and motives of the script were thrashed out.

It was at this point that Kennaway let it be known that he was both exhausted and stuck. "He just dried up halfway through," said Fisz. "It happens to a writer and he just can't go on. I was sorry for him. But things were desperate now. We just had to have a script. So we called in Paul Dehn to help us. He is a good writer. He had been intelligence officer during war. But he was like Jimmy and Guy when they came in. He didn't know score, didn't have background, and we didn't have time to let him find out. He did a first draft and then luckily James Kennaway got his second wind and went back to work."

By this time, though, two disasters had hit the film in quick succession, and both of them came without warning. On August 31, 1966, Freddy Thomas and Frank Poole, who is general sales manager of the Rank Organization, met Harry Saltzman and Ben Fisz to finalize the agreement for Rank's participation in *The Battle of Britain*. At this meeting Fisz was surprised and Saltzman considerably annoyed when Thomas informed them that he wished to alter the terms which Rank had previously suggested for their participation. He wanted much better terms for the overseas distribution of the film.

"Nothing doing," said Harry Saltzman. "You should stick to the terms you agreed to."

"Please," said Thomas. "Don't let me go back to my board of directors and tell them you have refused. I can't guarantee then that we will stay with the film."

He was almost in tears when the meeting ended, but he had got nowhere.

On September 9, 1966, Fisz received a letter from Frank Poole:

Dear Mr. Fisz,

BATTLE OF BRITAIN

I am confirming our conversation of this morning when I advised you that we have heard from Mr. Thomas, who has asked me to tell Mr. Saltzman and yourself that we are not prepared to move on the question of the commission overseas, and if this was still unacceptable you are quite free to make arrangements to make the film elsewhere.

Frank Poole

It was an ultimatum and both Fisz and Saltzman knew it. Fisz was for giving way at once. Saltzman was adamant. He sticks by his own deals when he makes them, and he expects other people to do likewise. He told Fisz to tell Rank they would not give way.

On September 23, 1966, they received the following letter:

Dear Harry and Ben,

BATTLE OF BRITAIN

There are so many differences between us regarding the proposed production that we have decided that the

Rank Organization do not wish to participate and accordingly we withdraw from the negotiations.

We regret the decision but should make it clear that it is final.

Freddy Thomas

"What do we do now?" asked Ben Fisz.

"We go to Paramount," said Harry Saltzman.

But at Paramount there were rebuffs waiting for them too. Saltzman had always been confident of his ability to make a deal with Paramount Studios, not least because he had a close friendship and a close working relationship with its chief, Howard Koch. But at the very moment that the negotiations were being broken off with Rank a revolution was taking place at Paramount, and a new king was ruling the kingdom. His name was Charles Bluhdorn.

One of the first things Bluhdorn did was to call a conference with Harry Saltzman in New York to find out what *The Battle of Britain* was all about. Other conferences followed in London. By the time they were over, Paramount too was no longer participating in the film. One of the chief reasons was a difference in temperament between the two men.

"What do we do now?" asked Fisz despairingly.

"We postpone the film," said Saltzman.

"Oh God," said Fisz. "After all I've done."

He was to say afterward that it was the worst moment of his life.

As It Was in 1940

By the beginning of July 1940, Reichsmarschall Herman Göring, supreme commander of the German Luftwaffe, was itching to unleash his planes and wipe out the Royal Air Force. As for his pilots, they were impatient to get into the air and do battle.

All the preparations had now been made for the onslaught on Britain. Three great German air fleets had been assembled in the occupied countries of Western Europe. Luftflotte 5 would operate from Scandinavia under the command of Generaloberst Hans-Jürgen Stumpff, with his headquarters at Kristiansand in Norway, a small force but with a useful backstop of long-range fighters capable of spanning the North Sea as far as Glasgow as protection for the command's bomber force. Luftflotte 2 would operate out of Belgium, Holland and northern France as far west as Le Havre under the command of Generalfeldmarschall Albert Kesselring with his headquarters at Brussels. This air fleet represented the major threat.

The third and final formation was Luftflotte 3 under the command of Generalfeldmarschall Hugo Sperrle with his headquarters at Chateaudun in France. Luftflotte 3 backed up Luftflotte 2 and its territorial area ran approximately from east of Paris westward to beyond the Cherbourg peninsula.

By July the air fleets in France, Belgium and Holland consisted of nearly 1,000 fighters (Me-109 single-seaters and Me-110 twin-seaters), 900 Heinkel, Junker and Dornier bombers, and 300 Junker Ju-87 dive bombers. The Scandinavian fleet had 123 bombers and 34 long-range twin-engined Me-110 fighters. It came to nearly 2,500 planes in all.

Against them the Royal Air Force had forty-six squadrons of Hurricane and Spitfire fighters, plus two squadrons of Defiants (which were hopelessly slow and vulnerable and soon shot out of the battle). The total came to about 660 single-engined fighters. It was almost a proportion of five German planes to one British plane, and as the c.-in-c. Fighter Command was saying about this time, when a minister was pessimistic about the outcome:

"Our young men will just have to shoot down their young men at a rate of five to one."

Fighter Command and the responsibility for the defense of Britain against the German onslaught to come was in the hands of Air Chief Marshal Sir Hugh Tremenheere Caswall Dowding. He was a remarkable man both in his knowledge of the techniques of air warfare and in his attitude to life and death. His nickname in the RAF was "Stuffy" and, in that ebullient service he no doubt earned it: he was a vegetarian, an introvert and a spiritualist. He did not drink. He did not consort overmuch with his fellow men. He suffered fools badly. He had so little facility for making friends that even with right and the facts on his side, he still contrived to make an enemy of Churchill, and failed to get the credit for his achievements in the Battle of Britain at the time.

Dowding's Fighter Command consisted of four operational groups whose planes were so disposed as to give protection to the whole of the British Isles. 13 Group under the command of Air Vice Marshal R. E. Saul was stationed at Newcastle and defended northern England and Scotland. 10 Group was commanded by Air Vice Marshal Sir Christopher Brand and had its headquarters at Box in Wiltshire, to defend the west of England.

But the two most important groups were 12 and 11. 12 Group had its headquarters at Watnall, Nottinghamshire, and its task was to meet attacks on the eastern counties of England from Hull southward, and all the great industrial complexes of the English Midlands around Birmingham and Coventry. 11 Group was responsible for the defense of London and the southeast coast of England along the Channel.

12 Group was commanded by Air Vice Marshal Trafford Leigh-Mallory and 11 Group by Air Vice Marshal Keith Rodney Park. In the coming battle, it was vital that they should fight shoulder to shoulder, for their boundaries of command were contiguous, and they would face the same perils in the days to come.

Unfortunately, Leigh-Mallory and Keith Park did not easily work together. This was to have important repercussions in the days to come.

II

Enter Adolf Galland

———◆———

"IT WAS ALL right for Harry," said Ben Fisz. "He had other fish frying—films already in production and several big projects for future. But *The Battle of Britain* was my life, and I couldn't let it die."

In the weeks following the announcement of the shelving of the film, a remarkable thing happened. Letters began to come in, most of them addressed simply to: The Producers, *The Battle of Britain.* They came in their thousands from all over Britain, but there were also hundreds from Australia, New Zealand, South Africa, Canada and the United States. Many of them contained money with which, they proposed, a fund should be started to get the film made. Others proposed the formation of a public corporation which would raise funds on the London Stock Exchange and promote the film through shares backed by the public, banks and private industry.

Fisz was convinced that he would get the film started in spite of all the setbacks, but only if he could keep together the nucleus of a production team which had been painstakingly built up since Harry Saltzman had come into the project. To his surprise, Guy Hamilton at once expressed his willingness to carry on working on the script and other directorial preparations. This was a gesture far beyond his contractual obligations and particularly touching since *Funeral in Berlin* had now been seen by other producers and offers were coming for him from British and American studios, all of which he turned down. He and James Kennaway went on working away at the script, which had now been finished several times but was being constantly reshaped and rewritten. Fisz's agent-in-charge-of-planes was still searching the world for World War II aircraft and incurring some considerable expenses, but not without results. And thanks to an air commodore at the Ministry of Defense (Air) named James Wallace, whose enthusiasm for *The Battle of Britain* had now caught fire, the Ministry of Defense had been prevailed upon to put on ice all the arrangements they had promised for cooperating with the production until such time as they were needed.

But would Harry Saltzman's enthusiasm remain high in spite of the rebuffs, and would he go on paying the now considerable bills being incurred for what the film industry was now writing off as a moribund project? This was a question which caused Ben Fisz many a sleepless night; unnecessarily, as it turned out, and a misreading of his partner's mind, for Saltzman never had any intention of abandoning the project. Even had his keenness lost its edge—and it never did—he would have gone on, if only to show the arrogant moneymen in the front offices of the big production companies that they could not thwart or intimidate him.

But this Fisz did not know. All he heard were rumors that Saltzman was being urged to get out before being financially engulfed by the growing expenses of a film that would never be made. It is a measure of his desperation, and also of his capacity to charm the birds off the trees, that he decided that only the government itself would persuade his partner to stick with him. Through his friend in the Air Ministry and the government, he pulled off an extraordinary *coup*. Mr. Denis Healey, minister of defense in the Labor government, was approached and suffused with such enthusiasm for the film that he sat down and, in his official capacity, wrote a letter to Saltzman praising him for taking such an interest in making the film of *The Battle of Britain* and expressing his warm admiration for his efforts to get it on the screen. At the same time, the deputy leader of the government in the House of Lords, Lord Shackleton, called a meeting of the Royal Air Force Association in the Houses of Parliament at which a resolution was passed urging that the film be made and nominating a committee to discuss how it could be financed.

Fisz said: "I was ready to try anything—without necessarily telling Harry what I was doing."

He did not, for instance, tell Saltzman that he was in the process of approaching the Rank Organization again in an effort to persuade them to change their minds. It was a typically soft-sell, Fiszlike ploy of the type which would undoubtedly have brought a snort of derision to Saltzman's nostrils. It started with a telephone call to Graham Dowson, the second most powerful man (under the managing director, John Davis) in Rank asking if they could have lunch together at Pinewood Studios. Dowson agreed. Then Fisz asked Lord Shackleton if he would join him and stress the RAF Association's interest in the film; and Shackleton also agreed.

When the date of the lunch came up, Shackleton had in fact flown to Aden to deal with the latest crisis in what was still a British crown colony, and Fisz went alone. But he was careful to stress Shackleton's interest in *The Battle of Britain;* he produced a copy of Denis Healey's letter; and then he went on to appeal to the Rank Organization's patriotism and to point out that if only they could come back and participate in the film, they would not only win the gratitude of the public, they would not only make money at the box office, they would not only be sponsoring a spectacularly exciting film, but they would not be forgotten when it came to rewarding those who worked for the nation. Who knows in what way gratitude might be shown?

Dowson wrote to Fisz a few days later to say that his organization was appalled to think that members of the government, members of the House of Lords and members of the press and public believed that Rank had withdrawn from the film willingly. They had always wanted to participate but they had had certain doubts about the script, and if only these could be resolved they would be willing to come back at once. Nothing was mentioned about terms of participation.

By this time, however, Saltzman had already washed his hands of Rank so far as participation in the film was concerned and, unbeknown to Fisz, was having talks of his own. It was 1967 by this time and, in addition to a director, a scriptwriter and a buyer of World War II planes there was already quite a tidy staff of experts attached to Spitfire Productions—an art director and several assistants, a production manager and his staff, and the nucleus of several other departments which would automatically expand if the film was made. The chiefs of all these departments were well aware that they were living on borrowed time and Harry Saltzman's money, and they were apprehensive about how long it would last.

"Then suddenly," said Ron Allday, who had been

appointed chief accountant to the production, "Harry called us all to this special meeting. The whole of the production staff were there and not one of us knew a thing. All we knew was that it was now a question of whether the film was ever going to be made or not. Everyone was very tense. We had been warned that this was it—everyone would either get their notice at this moment, or the film was on. Well, Harry came bustling in. I didn't know him very well in those days and I couldn't tell a thing from his face. He said, 'Well, gentlemen,' and then turned at once to me and asked me how my wife was. He knew my wife was expecting a baby and so was his. I told him. He said, 'I love babies.' The next thing you know, everyone around the table is talking about babies, bringing out snapshots, talking about teething problems and what age they start to walk and talk. Honestly, it was crazy. Then after about thirty minutes of this, Harry suddenly said, 'Gentlemen, I think it's about time we wrapped up this meeting. We start making the film next year.'"

They all stared at him, but he was already on his feet and on his way out of the room. He did not bother to tell them that he had been to New York, that he had talked to United Artists and that he had made a deal. But what they did know was that, after all the trials and setbacks, *The Battle of Britain* was on.

All this time Guy Hamilton and James Kennaway had been hard at work on the script of the film, and it was already beginning to get a shape to it, though Hamilton was by no means satisfied yet. He has never been a documentary film producer and one suspects that he despises the kind of film in which fancy camerawork disguises the fact that what you are seeing is nothing but fish being landed in nets and mailbags snatched off posts by speeding trains. He was well aware that in making *The Battle of Britain* tough and realistic and true there was the danger that it could turn into a documentary, and that he was determined to avoid.

"All right, we are going to keep to the facts of the battle," he said, "and show it the way it was—really was, I mean, with real human beings flying those machines instead of starry-eyed knights of the air doing daring deeds to the sound of soulful music. All right, we are going to break a few eggs by showing for the first time some of the smelly things that were going on down below, in the Air Ministry, while the battle was being fought in the air. But we are also going to have people with whom audiences, particularly young audiences, can communicate and connect—fliers, airmen, their girl friends and wives—and they have got to give the emotion to our film. The audience, most of whom don't care a damn about the Battle of Britain as such, will have to ache, yearn, love and be scared out of their pants and miniskirts by what they see these people doing. And that ain't documentary, it's drama, and it's what we've got to get into our script."

What had to be got into the script, too, if *The Battle of Britain* was to live up to its claims, was a portrayal of the German side of the battle as truthful to the facts and as sincere in its drama as the portrayal of the British side; and it was here that Guy Hamilton realized that he might well face formidable difficulties.

Hamilton is a moody, introverted character who sometimes gives the impression of being as cold-blooded as a fish. He is fond of saying that he hates actors, but this he doesn't really mean, he married a very beautiful and temperamental example of the species and gives every sign of being very happy about it. But about the Germans he seems to be quite serious when he says he loathes them. Just why he is so emotional about them is not quite clear, except that he spent some of the most formative years of his life watching the way they behaved and hating them for it. He has been a Francophile since boyhood (his father was press attaché in the British embassy in Paris) and at the age of eighteen, while he was working as an office boy in the Victorine Studios in Nice and fan-worshiping its principal director, Julian du Vivier, the Germans overran France. He was evacuated aboard a collier and found himself sleeping "eight lumps of coal away" from a fellow refugee, Somerset Maugham. "He had had a fatal accident because he had lost the detachable collar to his shirt," Hamilton recalled, "and he looked incongruous with a gold stud keeping the top of his shirt together. And every morning, crunch crunch across the coal, would come his valet to wake him—*Good* morning, Mr. Maugham, and offer him a cup of tea from a bully-beef tin." From that moment on, Hamilton was always feeling the heavy hand of Germany; he was in the Blitz in London; he joined the Royal Navy and was in the famous PQ-17 convoy to Murmansk, Russia, which was all but completely destroyed by Nazi bombers, from which he transferred to the Mediterranean and the equally tragic "Ohio" convoy which was decimated by German bombers too. After that he was in motor torpedo boats running agents across the English Channel to France, and once spent a month in Occupied France watching the French under the heel of the Nazis.

At forty-six he still hates them. When Ben Fisz told him that all the German sequences in the film would be made in German with German actors (and English subtitles where necessary) he agreed at once.

But when he said that all the German sections of the script would be checked for accuracy by a German consultant, he said:

"That means trouble."

He was quite right. For the role of chief German consultant to *The Battle of Britain* Ben Fisz had chosen Adolf Galland. Galland was one of the great air aces of World War II, credited with shooting down 104 planes in the West, and twice winner of the Iron Cross for bravery in combat. Adolf Hitler pinned the second—an Iron Cross with cross swords, oak leaves and diamonds, the highest class of the order—on Galland's breast, but snatched it off again when he realized that the metal was gilded and the diamonds fake. He plucked the one hanging from Reichsmarschall Göring's breast instead and pinned it on Galland.* Generalleutnant Galland spent some time as a prisoner of the Allies, and under interrogation, after the end of the war and then emigrated to Argentina; but today he is back in Germany as a highly successful business consultant, principally in connection with the sale of aircraft.

He is a short, trim, dapper man with hair *en brosse* and a Groucho Marx-type moustache, and though fifty-six years old today he has changed little from the gallant, self-confident fighter-leader of the 1940s. He can be extremely pugnacious and argumentative when he feels that Germany's honor is being traduced, and he wages a personal crusade against the kind of films and plays made since the end of the war in which his people are portrayed as brutish Krauts or guttural figures of mockery.

---

* Who later handed it back to Göring in return for two in plain gold.

In addition to this, he made it clear when he was first approached to be a consultant on the film that he didn't believe that there was any such thing as the Battle of Britain, from which it followed that Germany certainly hadn't lost it.

"All that happened," he said to Ben Fisz, during their first conversation in Bonn, West Germany, "was that we made a number of attacks against England between July and September. Then we discovered that we were not achieving the desired effect, and so we retired."

Fisz regarded him with a bland smile. "Dear General Galland," he said, "have you ever been to boxing match?" When Galland nodded, he went on: "You know what happens when, in tenth round, one fighter is groggy on his feet and his trainer he leans over and throws in towel and shouts: 'My fighter retires!'? Who has won fight, general, and who has lost it?"

It is difficult, particularly for a German with Galland's background, perhaps, to see the amiable, flopsy figure of Ben Fisz as one of his opponents during the Battle of Britain; he does not look like an ex-fighter pilot and he reveals few details of his background. During their first meetings he must have seemed, to Galland, to offer an easy excuse for displaying the superiority of the man who was there toward the nonparticipant. It was a mistake which he only, it must be admitted, made once. It happened when he made his first trip to England to discuss the background to the film, and talk drifted toward the tactics and the strategy which the two sides had utilized during the battle. At one point Fisz asked Galland why the Germans had been so inept in their use of radar during the Battle of Britain. Galland gave him the look the expert reserves for the amateur.

"We didn't have radar," he said, stiffly.

Fisz: "If I may correct you, general, you had FREYA, which is what you called your radar. It was at the same stage of development as ours."

Galland: "Yes, but we didn't use it during the Battle of Britain."

Fisz: "You used it, general, but you didn't use it correctly. You had it on the French coastline, and you were tracking all our ships going into the Thames estuary, and that is why you were attacking our convoys during what we called the lull period in 1940. But you didn't use it properly."

Galland: "This is nonsense. It is not possible. We could not possibly have used it that way. Why, the curve of the earth would have prevented it. You are falsifying facts to try and make the Germans look stupid."

But forty-eight hours later, when Galland had returned to Germany, he sat down to write Ben Fisz a letter of apology. He had been completely wrong and Fisz was right, he wrote; from his inquiries he had ascertained that the Germans had indeed used their radar system in the way Fisz had indicated, the wrong way.

It was the beginning of a wary friendship, based on mutual respect, between the Polish Jew and the touchy German which was to be tested by several crises in the days to come. But toward everyone else, and everything else, connected with *The Battle of Britain*, Adolf Galland decided that he must act with suspicion and move with the greatest caution, and that he must be prepared to hit hard and shout loudly if he was to protect the interests of his beloved Germany in the forthcoming film.

"Do you mean I have to have a character like that look over the German sequences of my script?" asked

James Kennaway when he returned from a session with Galland in Bonn. The two of them had got on badly. Kennaway's questions to Galland had been too sharp—"loaded" was the word Galland used—and the German quickly suggested that a man with such a slanted mind was hardly the one to do justice to the German side of the story.

Fisz's attitude was both practical and simple.

"Dear boy," he said, "if you put anything in script about the Germans which is untrue, Galland will scream blue bloody murder and demand that we take it out. So we will take it out. We are trying to tell truth. But if you put something in script which is true and Galland screams blue bloody murder, we will scream blue bloody murder back at him. And we will not take out."

With that both Kennaway and Guy Hamilton had to be satisfied. Hamilton had his first meeting with Galland when he came to London in the spring of 1967 and it would be untrue to say that it was a case of love at first sight. The two of them spent part of the session banging the table at each other over certain aspects of the war, and the future of Anglo-German cooperation so far as *The Battle of Britain* was concerned was not auspicious when Galland flew back to Germany.

Nevertheless, toward the end of August 1967, a copy of the shooting script as Kennaway and Hamilton had shaped it at that date was dispatched to Adolf Galland and writer and director waited with glum foreboding for their German adviser's reactions to it. Their pessimism was justified. Galland's reaction varied between choler and disbelief. Was this the film about the Battle of Britain intended to do justice to both sides? Was this what the British meant by being fair?

Galland speaks English well, with only an occasional German inversion of a sentence and only the odd pause to pluck a forgotten word from his memory bank. He reads it well and knows all the nuances, and he writes it most competently. It seems from subsequent conversations with him that he read through the script he was sent on the evening that it arrived, and almost at once sat down at the typewriter to make his comments. These were devastating and are worth reproducing here. This was, of course, the script in existence in 1967 and those who have read it since are probably agreed that it was hardly up to its subject (this writer is, anyway), and it is interesting to see how a German searching for slights on his countrymen and fellow fliers also finds flaws which have nothing at all to do with either.

Galland wrote:

Already when first reading the script for information, one gets the impression that here again the chance is spoiled to make a true fliers', or better still, fighter pilots' film. What is planned is one of the usual solemn hero-worshiping films on the war with which the public is so fed up. The only attraction of the film might be found in the planned fights in the air, if they can be realized.

It was to be expected that this film would give a one-sided picture of the Battle of Britain purely from the British point of view. This battle has become a myth, but also a kind of trauma, to the history-minded Englishman. . . . The film is not even very English, for no attempt is made to toy with the famous English understatement, but it is simply heroic from beginning to end. The characters in the film do not know what fear is.

Having delivered his opening barrage, Galland proceeded to get down to particulars:

It could not be expected that this film would be partic-

ularly pro-German. On the whole the Germans are reduced to the role of mutes here; they have to provide the
cue to the British heroes for herolike behavior. Three cate-
gories of Germans have been set up.

1. The top-level leaders like Göring, Hitler down to
Kesselring, Milch and Jeschonnek. On the whole the men
in this category remain dull. They talk a lot of nonsense,
make many mistakes, but are not so much villains as
"little men" in uniform. Hitler does not appear . . . people only dare talk about him in whispers. Göring's part is
that of the always poorly informed, fat, mendacious-
jovial braggart who surrounds himself with oriental
splendor. . . . On the whole this menagerie of vanity
could be accepted. It is a matter of opinion.

2. The medium-level leaders. There are types like Fink,
Schmid (Smidt in the script) and Osterkamp (Oster-
kampf in the script). The characterization of this category
is definitely unlikable with the exception of the sarcastic
Osterkamp. Fink "an accurate, humorless, petit-bourgeois
man . . ." Schmid "a rather oily little intelligence major."
The question arises if it would not be better to let these
people remain as anonymous as the fighting soldiers, the
more so because Fink and Osterkamp are still alive.

3. The young pilots. This consists of a number of by no
means unlikable young officers. Overall impression: nice
fellows, not particularly brainy, big boys, whose aim in
life is another medal, all of them characters who could
have come out of the pen of a man from a propaganda
company in the year 1940, without any differences and
thus rather dull in spite of all the likeable traits, and
without any intellectual abilities.

For some pages Galland then proceeded to find and
angrily protest against what he believed were insults
to Germany and to the memory of his fellow fliers. It
was "unbearable," he declared, to have to read scenes
in which German bombers deliberately attack civilian
targets in London, and it was "a malicious distortion
of the truth. At no time in 1940 did German bombers

have orders to bomb only residential districts in London. Naturally many civilians were killed during these raids. But in the film it looks as though this had been done on purpose." He objected to the fact that in the script "the English smile and the Germans always grin," that in the scenes in which a thinly disguised version of himself is shown he always returns from a raid and asks for a bottle, and he was furious at one scene showing German pilots shooting down British pilots parachuting from their burning planes, "extremely malicious."

But all through his report he kept coming back to the overall spirit and feeling of the script:

From the point of view of a fighter pilot, I particularly miss the following aspects:

1. The enervating wait for the alarm, the sudden change from the mere killing of time with all sorts of games or just dozing to the hectic state of an alarm start. It does not become evident that the sounding of the alarm loudspeaker can also turn the stomachs of the ice-cold experts, for they are no superhumans after all. There are no moments of despair, fear, self-victory from which courage grows, but only stupid wordless heroics. Therefore, all fighter pilots on both sides to me seem to be only types, not human beings.

2. The peculiar sensation of flying over water, the uneasiness connected with it. It should by all means be shown that it means to jump from the aircraft into the canal [the English Channel] and to drift in the water for a few hours. . . .

Finally, one can only say: What a pity if one thinks of the money that it is going to cost. A useless film which can very well be made without German participation. Typical is the montage from horror shots toward the end of the film. After more than 200 heroic shots it must then be emphasized that "at heart one is also against war." Now, my dear young people, you watched with enthusiasm fights and victories for two hours, but during the next five minutes you will see how wicked it actually is. And besides, we won the war and swept the naughty Germans from the sky. Don't you ever forget that! And then: Never ever war again, because it is often lethal. And now music. Perhaps the *Warsaw Concerto*? "Kitsch as kitsch can."

Summarizing, I can only say that I do not think that this script could be altered to a great extent. Its tendency would have to be changed completely in order to make it acceptable also to a German. Let the British have their Battle of Britain, but spare us.

Fisz, Kennaway and Hamilton read the indictment through and then sat in silence for a time, looking at each other.

"That bloody German!" said one of them.

There was another pause, and then Guy Hamilton said:

"I think we had better take another look at that script."

Ben Fisz wrote to Galland on September 18, 1967:

Dear General,

Thank you very much for sending me all your comments and observations on the script.

As they are quite lengthy and involved, it will take us some time to digest them, and as soon as possible we will be in touch.

Thanking you once again.

Yours sincerely,
S. Benjamin Fisz

Meanwhile, Kennaway and Hamilton had gone back to work. And it was not just inaccuracies about the Germans that they were eliminating from their script.

As It Was in 1940

—————◆—————

The legend seems to have grown, particularly in Germany, that the reason why the Luftwaffe lost the Battle of Britain was because the British had radar and the Germans didn't. The truth is that both of them had it, but one used it and the other misused it.

The RAF had established a chain of radar stations all along the south and east coast of England from which they could "read" any signs of air activity over the German bases in France. The moment large forces began to rendezvous in the air behind Calais, RAF fighter squadrons were scrambled and sent up to meet them. Radar scanned the German bomber formations every second of their journey toward England, knew their height and direction, and were thus able to guide the British fighters to their target. To that extent the tactics of the British were controlled from the ground, even at the height of the battle.

The Germans, on the other hand, worked out a flight and battle plan on the ground before they took off, and then were on their own. They were, of course, not using radar to guide them. At first, they could not understand how the RAF always succeeded in finding them, even in the clouds. Their ace pilots, like Adolf Galland, heard voices in English giving instructions to the RAF pilots he was fighting, and sus-

48

pected that there was a controller guiding the British fighters, but where? It must sometimes have seemed to them that the RAF had some kind of superbeing on their side, flying above the battle and telling them what to do.

The Germans trained their radar sets on the water instead of into the air. They were looking not for planes but for ships. Thus, on the morning of July 28, 1940, General Johannes Fink, commanding the Luftwaffe operations over the Channel, received a message in his caravan on Cape Gris-Nez, in the Pas-de-Calais, to tell him that the German radar had spotted a British convoy off Southend, on its way out of the Thames. There were twenty-one ships. It took only a short calculation and consultation with the tide tables to tell him when it would pass through the Straits of Dover. He alerted his dive bombers, the Stukas which had done such devastating destruction and spread such terror in Poland and France.

The mist had cleared and the sun was shining when the convoy came into view off Dover. Fink gave orders for his Stukas to take off and for a covering guard of Me-109s to go with them. He then went outside his caravan to have a grandstand view of the attack, for he could plainly see the convoy across the water.

Meanwhile, at his headquarters at Bentley Priory, Dowding had been told that the Stukas had taken off —radar had spotted them. He ordered the RAF fighters aloft.

The subsequent battle was a mad hell of twisting planes, spouting water, noise, smoke and flame. Not only was Fink watching it. On the other side, English crowds had gathered to see the spectacle, like watchers at a firework display.

By the time the Germans were chased off, six vessels had been sunk and six damaged. A British destroyer had been put out of action. The Germans lost sixteen aircraft and the British seven.

Two future aces had flown against each other that day. One was Major Adolf Galland of the Luftwaffe and the other Flight Lieutenant Al Deere of the RAF.

III

The Leprechaun in the Bowler Hat

ONE FAMOUS FILM about bomber operations in World War II took most of its air battles from combat-camera shots of actual raids over Germany, altering its story to fit the kind of flying sequences the filmmakers were able to dig out of the archives; for scenes with characters on the ground, they used engineless full-scale models of the planes. Another air film managed to shoot all its flying sequences with the use of three aircraft only—and a good deal of ingenuity in the cutting room.

Since *The Battle of Britain* was to be a wide-screen production shot in color, clips from the actual Battle of Britain were unusable, a fact which did not, however, trouble Saltzman or Fisz. From the start they had planned to "re-create" completely the forty minutes of air battle which would be the spectacular high point of the film, using the same planes and simulating the same clashes which had once been fought over the English Channel and the Thames estuary.

But how many planes would be needed? And where could they be found?

In his early, optimistic days Ben Fisz had been convinced that the Royal Air Force would somehow be able to find the fighter planes he needed; they must have plenty of Hurricanes and Spitfires lying around, and they must also be holding on to at least half a dozen captured Messerschmitts. In fact they were able to provide *The Battle of Britain* with a number of Spitfires, some fliers, some runners and some non-starters suitable for dressing a set; but what about the Hurricanes, the Messerschmitts and the Heinkel bombers? No luck there.

This was where a character named Group Captain Hamish Mahaddie came in. He is a highly decorated (DSO, DFC, AFC and bar) bomber pilot from World War II and his speciality is buying airplanes for films. Mahaddie is so Scottish that it would be ridiculous were it not for the fact that he has turned his accent, his phraseology and his frequent references to "my Scottish nature" into a most engaging cover for shrewd bargaining in the curious marketplaces where airplanes are bought and sold. He is a small pink man with gray hair and bushy eyebrows which wag like semaphore flags when he speaks, and he is never to be seen without a black bowler hat which he either carries or wears square on his head; he takes it with him wherever he goes, be it a desert airfield in Syria, a marketplace in Seville or a snow-covered back lot in Germany. With his button-bright eyes, pink complexion, unquenchable energy and constant smile, he resembles a leprechaun dressed in his Sunday best, and when you meet him for the first time you expect him to burst into the theme song from *Finian's Rainbow*. His invariable reply to an inquiry as to his health is:

"I could burst a drum!" And when he takes your leave, he first looks you straight in the eye and asks: "How can I confuse you more?"

Mahaddie has green fingers where aircraft are concerned; he not only knows where to find them, but he also cannot be fooled about their condition. He made his way into the higher ranks of the RAF from the bottom as an engineering apprentice at Halton, and there is very little about the way a plane works or flies that he cannot tell you. As soon as he was given the assignment by Fisz to start buying planes, he began questioning his contacts at the Air Ministry and among the air attachés of every country where Spitfires, Hurricanes, Messerschmitts and Heinkels had operated. He started on the assumption that there were only about six Spitfires left in the world—and so did most of the people who owned them; they asked outrageous prices. Soon, however, he had tracked down no less than 109. "My Scottish nature being what it is, I not unnaturally had refrained from buying until I had my tallies in, and our initial expenditure was not as much as I had originally feared," he said.

But it was in the matter of Messerschmitts and Heinkels that the producers faced their most difficult problem, and Mahaddie his trickiest task. One of the most dramatic sections of *The Battle of Britain* is the bombing of London (the blitz) by hordes of German bombers in the summer of 1940, with Spitfires and Hurricanes attacking them and dogfights all over the sky with the protecting squadrons of Messerschmitts. How could this be shot if they only had a handful of planes? By doing the whole thing in the studio with models and trick photography? Everybody curled up at the prospect. It would look like a fake and it would put a blight on the whole film.

Then Mahaddie, who had been one of the first to contact Adolf Galland in Germany, confided his problem to the general and he at once came up with a solution.

"Why don't you try Spain?" he asked. "Their bomber force is composed of Heinkel bombers; though," and he sniffed lightly, "they use Rolls Royce mermaid engines in them nowadays instead of Mercedes Benz. Their fighter force used to use Messerschmitts, too— with Merlin engines also—but I hear they're scrapping them. They might let you buy them."

Mahaddie "scuttled for the telephone as fast as my wee legs could take me" and called his friends at the Air Ministry. There Air Commodore James Wallace put him in touch with the head of all the air attachés at the Foreign Office, who at once contacted the British air attaché, Group Captain R. L. S. Coulson, in Madrid. On January 21, 1966, Coulson wrote to Mahaddie to confirm that there were indeed Messerschmitts and Heinkels in Spain which might well be available:

Dear Group Captain,

I have now made further inquiries. The whole group of Messerschmitts are being dismantled with the exception of seven which will be put up for sale. The reason more are not to be repaired is because the engines Rolls Royce made are needed to keep the Heinkel-111s going. Some of the aircraft being dismantled would be useful for dress. All the seven being retained are, I am told, in excellent condition and will have flown only some two-hundred hours. . . . I have mentioned that you are a friend of mine and would be interested in buying one for your pri-

vate collection. The price would be about $6,300, which
is less than the propeller cost originally.

R. L. S. Coulson (Group Captain)

After consulting Fisz, Mahaddie wrote back to
Coulson and said his clients would like an option on
all the available Messerschmitts. On March 29, 1966,
he flew to Tablada, an air base of the Spanish air
force just outside Seville, and there was confronted
by an astonishing sight. In one of the hangars were
eight planes, all of which were more or less flyable;
but when he drove out to the other side of the airfield, on the banks of the Guadalquivir River, "there
was this enormous pile of scrap. I had a Spanish air
force officer with me and some Spanish noncoms, and
we picked around among the rubbage. By the time I
had gone through it all, I was astonished. There was
the material for a small air force lying around."

By this time Harry Saltzman had come into *The
Battle of Britain*, and when Mahaddie reported back
to London that by cannibalizing half the planes on
the scrap heap he could make up twenty planes,
Saltzman said:

"Hell, why not buy the whole lot? We're looking
for a whole German fighter force, not a squadron."

Mahaddie took another look. He decided that there
were the remains of about fifty planes lying around,
and out of those he could build about thirty viable
Messerschmitts.

"I'll buy the lot," he said, "How much?"

But it wasn't quite as easy as that. Under Spanish
law, all surplus material belonging to the armed
forces must be offered for sale to the general public,
and the system of sale is by a peculiar form of Spanish auction called a *sabasta*.

Hamish Mahaddie will remember that name until his dying day.

In the meantime, progress was being made on the bomber front too. It is one of the rules in Britain (and in most other countries, too) that service departments are not allowed to lend their official cooperation to the making of a film dealing with the armed forces unless they have first seen and approved the script. Nevertheless, both Air Ministry and Foreign Office officials went to work to help in any way they could, and in Spain between them they did a remarkable job. It was one of those periods when the Spanish government was once more working up agitation against British ownership of Gibraltar; tourists trying to get into Spain from the Rock were being held up for hours and days, British air services were being harassed, and Gibraltar's Spanish labor force was being intimidated. The newspapers were full of Spanish attacks on all things British.

It was at this moment that the British ambassador in Madrid, Sir Alan Williams, was persuaded by his air attaché that *The Battle of Britain* was in need of a helping hand. The ambassador spoke to Mahaddie and, on a subsequent visit, to Ben Fisz and finally sent an invitation to the Spanish minister for air asking him to lunch at the embassy. To his astonishment, the minister accepted, bringing with him one of his most powerful service assistants, Juan José Sánchez Cabal. The British diplomat talked for a short time about the film in which Mahaddie and Fisz were interested, and then turned the conversation over to Mahaddie. The Scotsman did some of the fastest talking of his life, telling the Spaniards something of the

Anglo-German background to the film, and ending by asking for the cooperation of the Spanish government. Could *The Battle of Britain* borrow the Heinkels of the Spanish air force, at a price, of course, to use in their film?

"I expected to have a glass of port chucked in my face, Anglo-Spanish relations being what they were at the time," Mahaddie said. "Instead, both the Spaniards heard me out and asked me questions. And then at the end, the air minister said: 'Write to us about it, Señor Mahaddie.'"

In fact it was Coulson who wrote the same day asking specifically whether the film company could fly with the Heinkels, photographing them in mass formation. He asked for permission for *The Battle of Britain* unit to use Málaga airfield, where the Heinkels were based, pointing out that they would be self-sufficient. He then once more stressed that the company would pay all expenses for the use of the planes, the fuel they used in their flights, and for the wages of pilots, crews and ground staff.

A week later Coulson received the following letter from the Spanish Air Ministry:

My dear friend,

In reply to your letter, I am pleased to be able to tell you that approval has been given by higher authority for the film company to take photographs of Heinkel aircraft in the air and on the ground. *At the same time, I am happy to inform you that all expenses incurred in the filming of the aircraft, i.e., the cost of flying, the cost of fuel and the maintenance of the aircraft will be completely free with the exception of the painting or changing of the markings on the aircraft.* [My italics, L.M.] However, I wish to say without prejudice that the producers at the end of the filming might wish to make a cash donation to the orphans' School of the Spanish air force personnel.*

I would be grateful if you could let me know when the film company will go to Málaga so that I can give the necessary orders to the appropriate authorities. I hope that I have been of some service to you and I await your further communication.

Juan José Sánchez Cabal †

It was henceforth to be known to the producers of *The Battle of Britain* as the $420,000 letter, for that is how much in the hire of planes the gesture by the Spaniards had saved them.

They now had the use of fifty Heinkel bomber planes, more than enough for the film company to bring to the screen their "re-creation" of the Luftwaffe's blitz on London during the Battle of Britain.

Now what they needed were the Messerschmitts.

The Spanish form of auction known as the *sabasta* is a system whereby all persons interested in buying the goods to be sold are first allowed to look them over and then put their bids in sealed envelopes which they hand over to the agent acting for the Spanish government. On the appointed day the potential buyers gather in the auction room—in this case a small shed just on the civilian side of the Tablada military air base—and the envelopes are opened. The highest bidder gets the goods.

Mahaddie had made several trips to Tablada and had picked out twenty-eight planes for which he wanted to bid, together with sets of spares and some useful scrap. He had talked to the air force colonel in

---

* They gave $1,400.

† Now Spanish air attaché in Washington.

The hunter and the hunted - a lone Heinkel III at the mercy of a Spitfire over southern England.

The waiting game - British pilots at readiness framed by the wing of one of their fighters . . . . .

. . . . . and in Northern France German Messerschmitt 109s camouflaged and dispersed round the perimeter of a temporary airfield await the order to attack.

Angriff ausführen - Messerschmitt 109s taxiing out to escort a daylight bombing raid on England.

Scramble - a Hurricane on the point of taking to the air against the invaders.

Contact - high over Southern England the climbing British fighters find the Heinkel bombers.

Fighter cover - above the bombers the escorting Messerschmitts see the rising attackers and pounce in defense of their charges.

The battle opens - a Messerschmitt closes in for the kill on a damaged Spitfire.

whose hands the *sabasta* had been placed and was reasonably sure that anyone else interested in the planes was only there for scrap, and that he would have no serious rivals. The fact that he was from a film company had been carefully concealed.

He arrived in Seville in mid-July 1966, on the day before the auction, and drove at once to Tablada air base just to see exactly where the shed was where the *sabasta* would be held. It was a blazing hot day. As usual, Mahaddie, who has a Scottish contempt for heat, was dressed in a natty black striped suit with waistcoat, a briefcase under his arm with certified letters of credit from the Bank of England, and the inevitable bowler hat on his candy-floss pink head.

"I got out of the car just near the edge of the military field," he said, "and started to walk toward a hut where they were obviously going to hold the auction. As I got near it, this draggety-looking character with a cigarette in his mouth came from the shady side of the hut and approached me.

He said: "Good morning, Coronel Mahaddie. I am from Madrid. I hear you need the planes here and want to buy them." He cut Mahaddie short when he started to talk and went on: "It is no use, we know all about it. You want the Messerschmitts. I thought you might like to know that I and my colleagues here"—and he pointed to a group of men who had now joined him—"have already bought them."

"You can't have bought them," Mahaddie said, crisply. "The *sabasta* isn't until tomorrow and the bids haven't been opened."

"No," replied the Spaniard, "but when they are you will find that our bid is above yours and the planes are ours." He paused to allow this to sink in, and then said: "But you do not need to worry about that. We are willing to sell them back to you for a million pesetas each."

It was of course much more than Mahaddie had promised to pay.

"I have never been more miserable in my life," he said. "I didn't dare take off my bowler hat because there was so much panic sweat inside it would have fallen over me like a shower. I was being held over a barrel—because I had to have those planes, and these keelies knew it. But if I had to pay their price, it would put nearly double my bill. So I stalled them, told them I would have to think about it, and went on into the military air base to meet my friend, the Spanish colonel, who was running the *sabasta*."

Mahaddie told him at once of his predicament. He waxed eloquent with indignation. How had these scoundrels learned about his interest, and how did they know how much he had bid for the Messerschmitts?

"Perhaps they do not," said the colonel. "Perhaps it is nothing but a bluff."

"There's only one way to find that out," retorted Mahaddie at once. "You have the sealed bids. You must open them and see if what those grave robbers out there say is really true."

The colonel drew himself up. "I am a man of honor, my friend. The bids are sealed. I could not possibly open them."

"Someone's obviously done it once, colonel, so why not again? Don't forget that I am a man of honor too, and my honor is now at stake. I have given my word to my friends in London that I will get these planes for them. And if I may say so, my honor is just as important to me as yours is to you."

Colonel: "My dear friend, we are both in the same cleft stick. Both our honors are at stake. We cannot do this thing."

Mahaddie looked at him for a long moment—and then walked away. He was in despair.

But the Scotsman had not gained his reputation in the film world for nothing. That night he was very busy. There were telephone calls—to London and Madrid, to his innumerable contacts in high and other places.

The day of the *sabasta* arrived. It was a hot day but there was no sweat under Mahaddie's bowler hat as he calmly took his place. His eyes were bright. His ruddy face had the confident, virtuous look of a man who knows that justice will triumph, that honesty pays and will be rewarded.

As indeed it was.

For when the envelopes were officially opened and the amounts read out, the rival syndicate's bid was found to have been unsigned—and therefore inadmissible.

Mahaddie has never revealed how he discovered his rivals' mistake. "It cost an awful lot in phone calls," is all he will say.

But his reputation was saved, the colonel's honor was saved. And the Messerschmitts were his.

By the end of 1967, Hamish Mahaddie had built up an air force strong enough to start a small war. He had the loan of fifty Heinkels of the Spanish air force, he had bought twenty-eight Messerschmitts, he had rounded up two squadrons of flying Spitfires (plus

the same number of "runners" for use on the ground),
and he had tracked down three, possibly four Hurricanes of which two maybe and one certainly could fly
(there were only six Hurricanes left in the world).*
The whole began to be known as Saltzman's private
air force.

Harry Saltzman was back from yet another visit to
New York and conferences with United Artists. He
announced that the budget for *The Battle of Britain*
had been agreed at $8,500,000, a figure at which the
members of the now rapidly expanding film unit
snickered quietly; they had all been on epics before
and knew how budgets can swell when they get out
on location.

The film now had a production manager with
enough experience to have given a guess, within a
few dollars and cents, of the eventual cost of the film.
His name was John Palmer and he was not unaware
of the snags nor ignorant of the haphazard nature of
the expenses on an enterprise of this kind. His last
two productions had been *Doctor Zhivago* and *Lawrence of Arabia*, both of which had had their imponderables. Palmer, a nut-brown, cheerful, bustling
little man with a penchant for blazers with brass buttons, is fond of enlivening the duller moments of studio conferences by discussing his relations with Sam
Spiegel, *Lawrence*'s producer, during the making of
that film.

"We were in Jordan," he said at one meeting,
"doing the big scenes with the Arab chieftains and
the camels. We had to have two thousand camels and

---

* One of the Hurricanes was bought as a job lot off a scrap
heap in Edmonton, Alberta, by an ex-Canadian air force pilot
who painstakingly rebuilt it and flew it across the Atlantic to
appear in the film.

we were offering the locals a dollar forty a day per camel for the hire of them. They were demanding four dollars. Just when I was digging my heels in the sand over the price, Sam Spiegel comes into the Bay of Akaba in that bloody great yacht of his, and the spokesman for the camel owners soon finds out all about it. 'How can you refuse us four dollars a day,' he asks, 'when your millionaire producer luxuriates in his yacht like that?' Well, he had a point, so I go to Sam and tell him what the man had said. Sam blows up into a fury. 'You go back and tell that bastard,' he says, 'that this isn't my yacht, it's my office!' "

Ron Allday, the accountant for *The Battle of Britain*, who also worked on *Zhivago* and *Lawrence*, breaks in:

"Did I tell you about the time when we moved the *Lawrence* unit to Spain and began shooting in Granada? There were those floods in England and terrible troubles with my new house, and to cap it all my wife had a miscarriage. I nearly had a nervous breakdown with worry, so I went to Sam and said I just had to get home for a few days. He was furious and I had to insist. He finally consented, but only after a big row. 'You know,' he said, 'your family troubles are giving me a real headache. What right have you to start a baby in the middle of my film?' "

Someone says: "Well, that's one trouble you'll never have with Harry. He loves the little bleeders."

"I'm going right back to start a baby now," says someone else.

Allday reported to Harry Saltzman at one of their regular meetings just before Christmas 1967 that *The Battle of Britain* was already costing $56,000 a week, and that this sum would start rising rapidly from now until March next, when shooting actually began. Then the cost would be more like $56,000 a day, not counting the stars, who had not been chosen yet.

Saltzman's reply to this was to bring a young American named David Haft into the production. He was a former garment manufacturer from New York who had made a million and then turned, with some success, to television. He was good-looking, eager, and ambitious, but he was not liked at all by Ben Fisz, who regarded him with deepest suspicion and considered him a potential usurper.

It took Haft some time to realize that though he would be looking after the second unit and the flying unit during the shooting of the film, he had really been brought in as hatchet man to keep down the costs—not exactly the role of a popular hero.

At a preproduction meeting at Pinewood Studios on Thursday, January 17, 1968, the state of preparations was set out as follows:

Producers:	Harry Saltzman
	Benjamin Fisz
Director:	Guy Hamilton
Production Supervisors:	John Palmer
	Sydney Streeter
Supervising Art Director:	Maurice Carter
Unit Production Managers:	Claud Hudson
	One other
Lighting Cameramen:	Freddie Young*
	Bob Huke (2nd unit)
Aerial Cameramen:	Skeets Kelly
	Johnny Jordan
Aerial Director:	Quentin Lawrence

* Another alumnus of *Zhivago* and *Lawrence of Arabia*, for each of which he was awarded an Oscar for his camera work.

2nd Unit Director:	David Bracknell
Principal Players:	To be advised
Starting Date of Shooting:	1st and 2nd units March 11, 1968. On location in Spain at Seville and San Sebastián.
Period of Shooting:	Starts March 12, 1968. Location period of shooting approximately five weeks. Combination of studio and English locations as from April 18 for approximately twelve weeks.
Information:	Construction work on Spanish location: The construction work occurs on three sites—Huelva Beach, Tablada and El Copero airfields at Seville (these airfields adjoin each other), and finally in the north of Spain in the area of San Sebastián. The work on Huelva Beach will consist of dressing the beach to resemble Dunkirk Beach with the aid of matte painting and requires the wreckage seen at Dunkirk to be strewn along several hundred yards of the beach together with an artificial sandbank beyond.*

At Tablada and El Copero airfields, which are under the control of the Spanish air force, we are to dress and camouflage various areas. . . . The aircraft on loan to us by the Spanish air force will have various

---

* A location-hunting crew under Maurice Carter and his assistant, Jack Maxsted, had picked Huelva for the Dunkirk beach sequence because of its sandy foreshore and its proximity to Seville, from which the main unit would be operating. It was only afterwards that they learned from the Spaniards that it was upon this beach that the body of The Man Who Never Was, dressed as a Royal Navy officer, false plans upon his person, was floated from a submarine in 1943 by British Intelligence to fool the Nazis. The corpse of the unknown Englishman who played the dupe is buried in Huelva churchyard. The Spaniards could not believe that the producer of the Bond films did not already know this.

German signs applied mainly by adhesive cutout letters. The gates of the airfield will be adapted with German signs and in the case of two buildings they will be dressed as an office and as a German fighter mess.

In the north of Spain, in the San Sebastián area, our main job will be to dress a small harbor and beach with barges and vehicles to simulate a port on the French coast in preparation for the invasion of England. . . . For scenes of Berlin by night we will be using the streets of San Sebastián and certain existing signs will be covered and special signs in German will be put up for shelters and subway stations. About an hour's journey away, it is intended to shoot Göring's Train Sequence, the train of which will be hired to us by Spanish Railways.

The first construction crews flew out to Seville from England on January 29, 1968. By March 11, they had been followed by a crew of eighty-five assorted propmen, carpenters, painters, signwriters, riggers, grips, makeup men and women, wardrobe assistants, hairdressers, accountants, camera operators, clapper boys, sound mixers, boom operators, art assistants, electricians, continuity girls and secretaries. By the terms of their union contracts, they had flown out first class by air to Seville (by a charter flight, but with caviar, pâté de foie gras and champagne en route) and were housed in the best hotels in Seville. ("Where it is unavoidable to share, individual members will be asked to make their own choice of room partners.") They would have an English-speaking medical attendant to look after them for the duration of the film, and an English catering firm would provide them with food (and wine, as it turned out) while they were on location. They would also be paid

$20.58 a week location allowance on top of their salary and overtime.

At the meeting on January 17, Guy Hamilton had reported that he was still working on the script, and pending his definitive version the art director, Maurice Carter, was not prepared to guarantee specific dates for specific scenes in Spain. In between his conferences with his artists at Pinewood, where a staff of twelve were drawing the buildings and choreographing the air battles which would eventually be used in the film, Carter was trudging over frozen British airfields with Hamilton which would be used later that summer for the locations of the British fighter bases, trying to picture how they would look under sunny blue skies. He was also attempting to keep a remote control, through Jack Maxsted, of the Spanish location work, "though I get so many distractions from the job in hand on things like budgets. (By the way, we had a meeting with Harry on Saturday and he did not press me too hard or brutally as to why the Spanish side was $123,000 over budget. For which I was duly grateful.)" This was on February 12, 1968. He added:

"Guy is still rewriting the script and we do not expect any of it until next weekend and without doubt every scene number will be changed. It's not possible otherwise, as there are so many additions, cuts and reassemblies."

At about the same time, one of his assistants, Lionel Couch, was writing to him:

I have not yet received one instruction that I can proceed with any of the English locations.

Unless we get these authorities to proceed during the next week, I cannot guarantee that I can prepare any of the airfields or London locations in time to meet the schedule.

Please understand that there is much work to be done before we can proceed on the site and that these authorities are now more than *most* urgent. Can I please have an answer?

There was a memorandum to Ben Fisz from Karl Fox-Dürring, a bilingual casting director who would be handling the German actors during the Spanish location sequences. He had found someone who, he believed, would make a perfect choice for the part of Göring. He lived in Hamburg, weighed 280 pounds, looked like Göring, and also sang in German musicals. His name was Hein Riess.

Fisz memoed back:

"Show him to General Galland. If he approves, he is in."

On February 28, Guy Hamilton and his wife left England for Marbella to spend some time at a beach house polishing up the script. Harry Saltzman had flown to Almería, in southern Spain, where another of his films, *Play Dirty* was just about to start shooting. David Haft was already in Seville. Ben Fisz was making final arrangements in London and endeavoring to tie down the stars he was trying to get for the leading roles in the film.

It was raining when Harry Saltzman reached Almería and the desert surrounding the town—which had simulated the Arabian wastes for *Lawrence* and would be the Western Desert in *Play Dirty*—was a mass of yellow mud, already sprouting flowers and grass.

Over in Seville, it was dry. But cloudy.

"Most unusual weather," the forecasters said at the Tablada Airport. "Truly, it is usually sunny at this time of year."

As It Was in 1940

On August 6, 1940, Reichsmarschall Herman Göring summoned his Luftwaffe commanders to a conference in Berlin.

Göring informed them that Hitler had made up his mind, England would be invaded at the end of September. But first the Luftwaffe must open the way.

"Your task is to destroy the Royal Air Force," he told them.

To do that, the tactics would be simple. First the RAF fighters must be brought up into the air and engaged in battle by the might of the Luftwaffe fighter squadrons. At the same time, all British radar stations (the Germans knew all about them by now) must be attacked and destroyed. And in addition, the airfields of the RAF must be put out of action, so that those British fighters which did escape annihilation would have nowhere to land.

The day of the great attack was to be known as Adlertag (Eagle's Day). He gave the date as August 10 (though in fact, because of bad weather, it was postponed to August 13).

From the lull before the storm which reigned over the Channel in the next few days, Dowding guessed Göring's intentions. An Order of the Day was issued to the RAF on August 8:

"The Battle of Britain is about to begin. Members of the Royal Air Force, the fate of generations lies in your hands."

Two days later it began, and on August 13 came the day of the great German offensive.

IV

The Rain in Spain

———————◆———————

I DROVE FROM France to southern Spain over the
weekend of March 10, 1968, and read en route what
was now called the final-final script (but there would
be still more changes). It had undergone considerable, even fundamental alteration since I had last read
it and now had the bite, the irony and the sense of
realism which had been missing in the earlier version;
it seemed unlikely that Galland, when he read this,
would persist in his objections to its sentimentality or
its romantic heroism. True, there was one British
character, a pilot, who seemed rather too decent and
daring to be true, but there were already rumors that
Robert Shaw had been offered the part and had consented on condition that he could do some drastic rewriting.

The conception of the story of *The Battle of Britain*
is an interesting one, but a tricky one to achieve. For
its scenes in the GHQs and the corridors of power on
both sides of the Channel during the battle, it had
been decided to portray actual characters and use

their real names. Reichsmarschall Herman Göring, Commander-in-Chief of the Luftwaffe, would appear in a particularly important sequence and so would Milch, Kesselring, Fink and Osterkamp (who commanded the German fighter forces in the West). The head of Fighter Command, RAF, during the battle was Air Chief Marshal Sir Hugh (later Lord) Dowding and he would play a large, a decisive role in the film, as would his two subordinates, Keith Park and Leigh-Mallory. A serious attempt would be made to show these men as they really were during the critical moments of the battle and of their lives; which meant that Göring, for example, would not, as Galland feared, be shown as a comical clown but as an approximation of his real and remarkable self.

Among these characters, plucked as it were from the pages of war histories and battle archives, it was inevitable that Dowding should be given the major attention. Here truly was a man of heroic and yet tragic proportions; the architect of victory in the Battle of Britain who, even in the midst of it, was the object of a mean-minded intrigue; whose reward for having beaten back the German attack and forced Hitler into abandoning the invasion of Britain was to be summarily retired at the end of it. (He still remains the only active British commander of the air forces during World War II who was overlooked when the monarchy appointed the rest to be marshals of the Royal Air Force.)

It is a choice role for a good actor, especially since the fires that evidently burned in Dowding's breast during the Battle of Britain were rarely visible on the surface; he gave (and gives) the impression of being a cold, austere, remote man, and therefore a real challenge to a sensitive actor searching for the key to his personality. At first Sir Alec Guinness had been offered the role, and had twice visited Dowding at his home in Tunbridge Wells to talk to him. He came back excited by the prospect of getting this complex character onto the screen. Alas, when *The Battle of Britain* was postponed Guinness's other commitments supervened, and he had to give up the role. There was now talk of casting Sir Laurence Olivier instead.

For the actual fliers in *The Battle of Britain,* and for their wives and girl friends, it had been decided that an amalgam of several personalities and types should be used rather than actual people; though audiences would be forgiven if they suspected that a character called Skipper with a very rough manner sounds like the late "Sailor" Malan, and that the German ace who likes to smoke cigars, especially after a sortie, though called Falke in the film behaves very much like Adolf Galland. There would even be those who think they see a real-life character in Maggie Harvey, the big female role in the film, that of a section officer of the WAAF (Women's Auxiliary Air Force), and wife of a Battle of Britain pilot. In fact, however, to give the scriptwriter room to motivate, to pry into their private lives, to inject emotion, to dig beneath the skin into their hearts and heads, all those characters have been made deliberately fictional. There was really no other way.

7:45 a.m. on Tablada air base and so misty that the nearby suburbs of Seville are blotted out and even the hangars on the edge of the field are all but shrouded from view.

It was March 13, 1968. I parked the car on the tarmac and walked across the grass, through a flock of

nibbling sheep, toward the sound of voices and revving engines. Suddenly out of the mist I saw the
shapes—two lines of Heinkel bombers, drawn up wing
to wing. As I got nearer the lines got longer, at least a
quarter of a mile of them, and now I could see the
bright blue of their undercarriages, the black wing
tops, the German crosses on the sides and the swastikas on the tail. It was a jolting sight for anyone with
memories of World War II.

High above the lines of planes a camera had been
fixed to the platform of a Chapman crane, so that it
could shoot down upon them when General Milch arrived in his Mercedes to inspect them. For the moment, however, it was untended. Freddie Young (the
lighting cameraman) and Guy Hamilton were in a
group just below it, flapping their hands and stamp-
ing their feet against the morning chill. A few yards
away Harry Saltzman, in his usual natty three-quarter
boots, a sweater, a windcheater and tight gray trousers, was standing with David Haft, who was wearing
a red sweater. The call sheet for the day had opened
with the announcement:

IMPORTANT NOTICE

At 8:00 a.m. precisely a one-minute silence will be ob-
served in memory of Don Federico Eglesias Lanzos who
died on Saturday, January 20, while flying an ME-109
from Tablada.

1. For the unit in the vicinity of the camera, one whistle blast will signify the start of the minute, two whistle
blasts will signal the end.

2. For the people not near the shooting area, a red
Very light will signal the commencement of the silence.

Lanzos was to have been one of the Spanish fliers who

would fly a Messerschmitt for the battle sequences
during the film, but he had crashed while doing acro-
batics on his own. Much to the astonishment of the
Spanish air force, the film's insurance company had
paid his widow 3,000,000 pesetas ($43,000) in com-
pensation. It may not have persuaded the other pilots
to follow Lanzos' melancholy example, but it had considerably eased their minds about the job they had
undertaken.

The whistle blew just as I reached the plane, and a
Very light flared in the misty air, throwing a red glow
over the fuselage of the bombers. The first assistant,
Derek Cracknell, a cheerful Cockney in a German
forage cap, raised a bullhorn to his lips.

"All right, fellas, cut the cackle," he shouted. "This
bloke's dead, remember?"

A heavy, self-conscious silence fell over the field
until the bullhorn spoke again:

"All right, fellas, let's get back to work. We've got a
long way to go."

Rehearsals began for the scene which runs behind
the credit titles of *The Battle of Britain,* and it soon
emerged as a triumph of organized coordination as
well as a spectacular shot. Men with walkie-talkies
were everywhere, and all cues were given by radio. I
began to wonder how Cecil B. De Mille ever did
without it. As the camera pointed down the long rows
of bombers, a radio call ordered the pilot of a revving
Junker trimotored bomber to taxi into view. At the
same time, a cavalcade of old German wartime cars
raced toward it and a squad of German soldiers
formed up outside it as it halted, its door opened and
General Milch stepped down. After which the cavalcade of cars drove swiftly between the bombers and
the inspection of planes and crews began.

The part of Milch is played by Dietrich Frauboes, a tall, handsome man with gray hair and leonine appearance. He proved as dignified offset as he did while acting, but with much more charm. The British company were a little wary of the German actors when they first appeared in Seville, especially in their Nazi uniforms, but they quickly thawed when they realized that they were actors first and Germans second. They warmed to one particular actor who had explained to them, over a beer the previous evening, that he was a Quaker and a pacifist, but was always playing generals in films.

"It's all due to my education," he told them. "I had a beast of a teacher at school who used to beat me and then make me stand to attention for hours whenever I slumped in my seat. Now I can't stand any other way. I *look* like a soldier. It's terrible, isn't it? But I always try to take the part of a really nasty kind of soldier—so that the audience will hate me, and perhaps in that way come to hate war too."

What made the *Germans* feel uncomfortable was a quartet of Texans who joined the unit in Seville some weeks before shooting started, and became the talk of the town from that moment on. They were four colonels and all veteran fliers from the U.S. air force: Lloyd Parker Nolan, Marvin Lee Gardner, Gerald Martin and Wilson Connell (Connie) Edwards. They got into the film because, back home in Texas, they run the Confederate air force, an organization which collects and flies aircraft from World War II. They had Spitfires and Messerschmitts that *The Battle of Britain* needed, and made a bargain in return for hiring them out—that they be among the pilots who flew them in the air battles. So they were cast immediately as Luftwaffe colonels.

Thereafter, they strode about the airfield in their uniforms, Iron Crosses round their necks, swastikas on their breasts, giving everyone stiff Nazi salutes, crying "Heil Hitler" and talking a cod German with a heavy Texas drawl. You could see the German actors cringing as they listened. Nor did they look any less uncomfortable when, between flights, Connie Edwards crossed his jackbooted legs and began to strum Mexican love songs on his guitar.

The Spaniards, particularly the girls and the small boys of Seville, much preferred the Texans in their Confederate air force uniform—black ten-gallon hat, khaki shirt and pants, and high-heeled black boots with silver spurs. They followed them through the streets as if they were film stars. On the other hand, when one day they walked back to their hotel in their Nazi uniforms, no one took any notice.

The rehearsals went on all morning while the crew waited for the light to improve. At three o'clock in the afternoon, the clapper board came up and Guy Hamilton cried "Action!" in earnest for the first time.

When it was over, Jack Maxsted of the art department touched his forelock.

"That's one shot done," he said.

"That means we've only another five-thousand-odd to go," said one of his assistants.

"It's a long, long road," said Maxsted. "A long, long road."

Guy Hamilton had climbed down from the crane and was pacing up and down, worrying about his next angle. He wore a small round canvas trilby on his head and he towered above the camera crew milling around him. I noticed for the first time that when he walks he leans forward at an angle, as if breasting a wind, his head at least six inches ahead of his feet.

He also clasps his hands behind his back. From a distance he looks extraordinarily like a medium shot of Monsieur Hulot in one of the films by Jacques Tati.

I thought it better not to tell anyone, particularly Hamilton, about this impression.

I dined that night at the Burladero restaurant in Seville with Saltzman and Hamilton. They had brought their wives along with them, and once the restaurant began to fill up, about 11 p.m., we got plenty of admiring glances, for the two women are slim, elegant and immensely attractive. Jackie Saltzman is a Romanian with wide, deceptively innocent eyes and an outward docility that conceals depths of energy and determination. She still travels on the Nansen passport she was given when she fled from Bucharest and the Russians after the war. She would like to have a Canadian passport too, like her husband.

"But I would have to stay in Canada for six whole months," she said. "I keep asking Harry if he'll come with me and the children—but can you imagine Harry staying six months anywhere?"

I suggested that she could go there on her own, and she replied by giving me a long look. She leaned across to her husband.

"Chéri," she said, "why can't you find a big, exciting film to make about Canada?"

"There aren't any, chérie," he replied. "It isn't that kind of a country."

Hamilton's wife is the only woman I have ever known whose nostrils actually flare when she is angry or indignant. Animal terms are, for once, apt to describe her, for she moves her lean body with a lubricated, feline grace. Her name is Kerima. Filmgoers will remember her as the lovely native girl in Carol

Reed's film version of the Conrad story, *Outcast of the Islands;* it was during the making of the film that Hamilton, who was assistant director to Reed, first met her. She is, in fact, South American though she was brought up in Paris, where her parents still live. Her sculptured face is arrogantly lovely, and her manner toward Hamilton fiercely protective. Like Jackie Saltzman, she does not like to be far away from her husband, especially when he is on location. "He must have someone to bring his troubles home to," she said.

We talked in French about anything but films while the meal was being served. Saltzman picked at his langouste but rarely put a mouthful to his lips, and I decided he had lost his appetite; I was to learn that, so far as meals in public places are concerned, he eats by sight rather than by mastication. He orders, he looks, he takes an occasional taste of his wife's choice, and then sends his own away.

Suddenly we were talking in English about *The Battle of Britain.* One sensed at once the unspoken tensions which must inevitably create a love-hate relationship between producer and director.

"What I've got to keep in my mind all through this picture," Hamilton said, "is that it should be strong—strong all the time, no softness in it."

"You can't keep emotion out of it all the time," Saltzman said mildly.

"I mean," went on Hamilton, as if he hadn't heard, "what we must keep emphasizing is that all through the battle a very dirty power game was going on."

Saltzman (again very mildly): "All right, but don't let's stir up too many wasps' nests. We're relying on RAF cooperation, remember."

Hamilton: "We don't have to worry about the RAF. They need our film more than our film needs them."

"Chéri," broke in Jackie Saltzman, suddenly, "what do you call crème Chantilly in Spanish?"

"Crème Chantilly," Saltzman said.

Kerima stretched over and stroked the back of Hamilton's hand with her long fingers.

Next morning the weather had closed in on the Tablada air base and not only was flying off for the day but the light was too bad for Hamilton to make follow-up shots of Milch for his title sequence. The crews stood around in groups, telling each other jokes, tossing pennies, waiting with the patience of long experience for the skies to clear. The bar of the flying club, on the civilian end of the field, was doing a roaring business among those who could get away from the set.

Harry Saltzman arrived in a yellow windcheater. He had been on the telephone to Almería to get a progress report on *Play Dirty*. The film had already had its share of crises, having lost one of its principal stars (Richard Harris) and its director. Now it was pouring rain in Almería.

"Geez," Saltzman said, "there's never been a spring like it in southern Spain before. They'll be growing wheat in that desert around Almería if this goes on."

"How's Michael doing?" asked David Haft, referring to Michael Caine, a protégé of Saltzman's, who was starring in *Play Dirty* and would be playing in *The Battle of Britain* as well.

"He should worry," someone broke in. "Brigitte Bardot's filming in Almería, and she's been rained out too."

Everyone laughed except Saltzman, who looked worried—mostly about the Spanish telephone service, as it turned out. For a man who calls four or five different countries several times a day, he was finding the long waits and bad lines frustrating. But when he came up to Guy Hamilton I noticed that his face lit up and his mood was cheerful, as if he had deliberately changed his emotional gears. While the two of them were together, Hamilton could not have guessed that Saltzman had anything on his mind but his director's immediate problems.

Presently Saltzman came over to me and asked whether I would like to drive across country with him. He was going to look at a farmstead near the Guadalquivir River which had been chosen as headquarters of one of the German fighter squadrons. We climbed into the back of a chauffeur-driven car and set off across the mustard fields along a narrow, bumpy road. It soon became apparent that the Spanish driver had not the least notion of where he was supposed to take us, but Saltzman seemed not to notice; he was busy talking. I asked him why he had run away from home and he said:

"I had two older sisters and two younger brothers, and I was the one in the middle. The one in the middle always gets squashed. I suppose the real cause was my eldest sister. She had this bicycle my old man had given her. I liked riding but she wouldn't let me touch it, and every time I sneaked a ride she would tell the old man, and he would give me a beating. Then one day when everyone was out and I was sure no one was looking, I took the bike and went for a ride. When I got back there was still no one around. I was safe. I put the bike back where I'd found it. But that night I got a beating from the old man, just the same. My sister had put a pencil mark on the wall exactly where she'd leaned the handlebars, and I hadn't noticed. I think that was the time I decided I'd better clear out."

He was silent for a time while his mind chewed on a memory which was evidently still bitter. The driver had slowed down the car now because, just ahead of us, the hull of a large ship seemed to block our way; it was, in fact, a merchantman on the way down the Guadalquivir to the sea.

"Señor," said the driver, turning, "where you want me to go?"

"Foehn's headquarters," said Saltzman, giving the name of the farm in the film.

"Foehn?" The driver repeated the word several times. "What means Foehn?"

"Hell," said Saltzman, "didn't anyone tell him where to go?" He gabbled something in Spanish and the driver shrugged and began to drive on, muttering, but Saltzman paid him no attention. He asked me about a book I had just finished about Germany in the two years before World War II.

"Did I tell you I was in Germany in 1938?" he said presently.

"That can't have been comfortable," I said. "Not for a Jew."

"I was working for this variety agency in Paris," he said. "We had forty theaters all over Europe—in Hungary, Romania, Austria, Poland, Germany, Switzerland, Scandinavia, Holland and Belgium—and we were constantly shuttling acts and circuses from one to the other. By 1938 we had about two million marks in the banks in Berlin, and then suddenly Schacht came along and blocked them. We couldn't get the money out. So I said I'd go to Germany and try to do something about it."

We had come to a halt in a small Andalusian hamlet full of grubby children, muddy geese and broken-down hovels.

"Señor," said the driver, "you tell me where we want to go, and I ask this lady here."

"How the hell should I know where we want to go," Saltzman replied. "All I know is the name of the place in the film. Look for a farm—any farm—it should be round here somewhere."

We plunged on down an increasingly potholed road.

"You know the first thing I did when I got to Berlin?" Saltzman asked. "Well, actually the first thing I did was to book into the Adlon Hotel. But after that I started buying tickets—railway tickets, wagon-lit reservations, steamship tickets. All through the summer of 1938, I had every act we handled travel through Germany from one theater to another. If they were coming from Hungary to Poland, they bought international tickets to the Austrian frontier—after which I had someone hand them German tickets, bought with German marks, to take them to the Polish frontier. I bought steamship tickets on German ships from Trieste to Hamburg, from New York to Rotterdam, wherever there was a German line going that could take an act, a chorus, a company of acrobats and their families, or a circus."

In this way he had whittled the agency's holdings down to a nominal sum. With some of the residue he bribed minor Nazi officials to provide *Ausweisen* (exit permits) for Jewish variety artists trapped in Germany.

"There was this Dutch acrobat, a queer," he said, "who used to hang out at Florence's, a supper club where all the foreign artists used to meet. You gave him a few hundred marks and he could get you a pass to anything."

"Señor." The car had come to an abrupt halt at the edge of the river. We could see a narrow road on the other side and a farm beyond it, but there was no bridge in between. There was no other way to go but back, but the driver needed to be told. Saltzman told him.

"Then one morning," he went on, as if he had never been interrupted, "the Gestapo knocked on my door. It was about six a.m. I thought they'd come about the *Ausweisen* in which case I was in real trouble. I decided it was a moment to bluster. I shouted that I wasn't coming out until I was dressed, bathed and shaved. I said how dare they come at this hour to the room of a foreign guest. To my amazement, it worked. They said they would go downstairs and wait for me. I dived for the telephone and called the Canadian and the French embassies. When I got down at eight o'clock, there was a vice-consul from each waiting for me. It turned out that the Germans weren't the Gestapo after all, but police sent by the treasury. They'd come to inquire about all that ticket buying, and warn me that it had to stop. I promised that it would—I didn't have many more marks anyway."

He laughed. "D'you know what happened that night? I went round to a vaudeville theater and was going backstage to see an act when the manager stopped me and asked me what I wanted. I told him. 'What do you want to see them for?' he asked 'They aren't Jewish. That's all you're interested in—getting Jews out of the country.' I said, 'If you know that much, you must be a member of the Gestapo.' He drew himself up. 'I've been a member for seven years,' he said. 'It's time you got out of Germany, Harry. This morning it was only railway tickets. But next time, it will be *Ausweisen*—and that's different.' I left for Paris next morning."

We were back on the main road to Tablada now. The skies had cleared and the sun was beginning to shine. Suddenly over on our left we saw a marvelous sight. A formation of light blue Messerschmitts was flying over the fields toward us. The driver began to laugh and shout with pleasure at the sight of them. Saltzman gazed at them morosely.

"Funny thing," he said. "I ran into that manager again a couple of years ago. He's living in Madrid. He asked me for a job."

He didn't tell me what he had said to that, and I didn't ask him.

When we got back to the airfield Claud Hudson, the unit production manager, ran across to us.

"We've just heard from London," he said. "The B-25 is coming in this afternoon."

The B-25 was the World War II Mitchell bomber which had been adapted as a camera plane and would fly with the fighters and bombers during the air combat sequences.

"Good," said Saltzman. "Let's hope the weather behaves itself."

As if in reply to him, the sky almost immediately clouded over and it began to spit with rain. He shook his head in mock despair.

"Another thing," said Hudson. "We've got a visitor tomorrow from Germany. General Galland is flying in."

"What time?" asked Saltzman.

"The afternoon, I think."

"Then I'll miss him," Saltzman said. "I'm going back to London in the morning." A long pause, and then he said: "A pity."

As It Was in 1940

On August 21, 1940, Reichsmarschall Herman Göring arrived on a visit to his air fleets in France, and he was in a rancorous mood. Eagle's Day and the attack which followed it had not gone off as well as had been planned. For five days the fighter pilots of both sides had been exhausting themselves in constant dogfights over the Channel and southeast England. The Luftwaffe had been flying more than 1,500 sorties a day, and the RAF as many as 700.

There had been grievous losses on both sides, and the RAF was now desperately short of planes and pilots, particularly pilots.

Both sides had, however, exaggerated their successes, to such an extent that America (still a neutral country with correspondents on both sides) had begun to charge the British with grossly inflating their claims and concealing their losses. At this time they chose to believe what the Germans were saying about their triumphs in the air.

This worried Churchill. He sent his secretary of state for air to Dowding to ask him whether he was exaggerating or not.

"I replied," wrote Dowding, "that the Americans would soon find out the truth; if the Germans' figures were accurate they would be in London in a week, otherwise they would not."

Unfortunately for Göring, however, he had believed the German figures. The RAF had been wiped out completely, according to these. Save for a few odd planes, there was no more opposition. So he took two decisions, one of which was wise and the other fatal.

He ordered his Stuka dive bombers to be taken out of the battle. He was right; they were too vulnerable and were being knocked down like ninepins.

He also ordered the attacks on the RAF radar stations to be called off, on the grounds that it was impossible to put them out of action, and that they were not important anyway. In fact, one radar station had already been destroyed and blown a great gap in the RAF protective screen. Had the Luftwaffe gone on for another week attacking the others, they would undoubtedly have knocked them out, "blinding" the RAF, which would henceforth have had to fight in the dark, with no far-seeing eyes to watch the enemy coming in to attack.

Now, during his tour of his Luftwaffe squadron, Göring discovered exhaustion and low spirits where he had expected high morale. He now knew that the figures were wrong, that the RAF was still up there in the sky, and he blamed his pilots for it.

"Göring came to inspect us and stayed to insult us for more than an hour," recalled Galland. The German ace was tired out from constant sorties in which he had made the salutary discovery that the Spitfire was a faster and more maneuverable plane than the Me-109: it could turn tighter and get on your tail if you were not ultra careful. His own brother had been killed a few days earlier because he had made that discovery too late.

Now, when Göring angrily shouted: "You have the best aircraft in the world," and added: "What more do you want," Galland had replied:

"A squadron of Spitfires."

But if the RAF was still flying, it was nevertheless in a poor way. It had been badly wounded by the Luftwaffe in the battles following Eagle's Day, and Dowding was afraid that if something wasn't done soon, the RAF would bleed to death.

V

The Psychedelic Monster
and the General

THE ARRIVAL OF the B-25 Mitchell bomber at Tablada air base is a memory which all of us who saw it will savor for a long time. It came out of a cloudy sky in the early afternoon of March 18, 1968, and circled the field about five hundred feet up. The day was gray, but the B-25 brought its own colorful brand of sunshine: its tail wings were electric green and the body half-green, half-red, the wings were striped in yellow and black, the engine cowling was yellow and white, and there were great plexiglass bulges on its nose and along the top of the fuselage.

"It's a bloody great psychedelic monster!" cried Derek Cracknell, the assistant director, as it came into view, and the Psychedelic Monster it was christened from that moment on.

One turn of the field, up into a cloud and then whoosh! in it came, at a howling speed and not more than twenty or so feet above our heads—a smear of multicolored paint on the palette of the sky. All over the field, airmen were throwing themselves flat on their faces.

Its pilot, John R. Hawke, had been preceded by his reputation, and we already knew quite a little about him. He had been a pilot in the RAF and a member of that service's famed aerobatic team, the Red Devils. He had caused the United States some embarrassment during the early days of his service by chasing a fast, high-flying object over his base in Cyprus well into Turkey and the frontiers of the Soviet Union, only to be called off when the British found he was "shadowing" the first of the U.S. U-2 spy planes. His first job after he left the RAF was to pilot a two-seater Messerschmitt across the Atlantic with his fiancée (later his wife) in the spare seat; after which he had settled in Fort Lauderdale, Florida. And there he had embarrassed the U.S. for a second time by taking a job ferrying surplus B-26 bomber planes from America to Portugal. The American government had agreed to abide by a United Nations resolution not to supply military planes to colonial powers likely to use them in Africa, such as Portugal; but when Hawke had his eighth delivery impounded on the airfield of Portland, Maine, and was subsequently charged with smuggling military weapons out of the country (this was in 1966), he vigorously maintained that he had been hired to do the job by the Central Intelligence Agency (CIA). At the subsequent trial, the CIA equally vehemently denied that he was working for them, and a key figure with whom he had done the original deal vanished without trace.

Nevertheless, Hawke had been acquitted. He told the court some thrilling stories about code names which he had been given by his employers while in flight, one of which was "Sparrow." During one mission, he explained, he had had engine trouble and had strayed from his flight path while passing over Washington; he did not realize that he had crossed into the forbidden zone over the White House until the air came alive with aircraft and he was escorted down to Washington National Airport. He realized that he was in big trouble. Everyone thought that he was planning to bomb the president. So, tentatively, he mentioned the code name "Sparrow." There were telephone calls, changes of attitude, and Hawke was soon on his way.

The jury believed him, even if the U.S. government continued to deny that he was working for their intelligence service, and he was acquitted. Not only that. A year later he owned two B-25 bombers himself, but had learned a salutary lesson; he wanted these to be used for photographing films.

Knowing all about this colorful background, it was disconcerting to discover that Hawke was only thirty years old; but his appearance certainly lived up to his record. He looked rather like a well-fed Mephistopheles in a touring opera company. He had a barrel-shaped figure, an untidy crop of hair and a jet black spade beard. His eyes were bright as polished buttons and when you looked into them, you always got the feeling that though his expression was serious he was secretly laughing at you.

Between them, Hawke and the producers of *The Battle of Britain* had turned the Psychedelic Monster into a remarkable flying studio, as I was to discover when I flew with it next day. There had been a briefing in the morning for the thirty-odd pilots of the Heinkels that were to be used that day, plus the pilots of fifteen Messerschmitts who would act as their escort.

Someone had drawn chalk marks over the floor of the hangar—which other people scuffed out as they walked over them—and small models of bombers and fighters on the ends of sticks had been placed over them. On the wall was a blackboard filled with the choreographic patterns of the various maneuvers which the film unit director was (hopefully) planning to get into his camera.

The expert in charge of the flying sequences at this stage was a man from the Royal Aeronautical Club named John Blake, a brisk but amiable man with one arm, a handlebar moustache right out of a wartime caricature of an RAF type, and a voice as crisp as a pruner clipping rosebushes. He bustled in front of the forty Spaniards, half a dozen Englishmen and four Americans who were assembled for the briefing and inevitably began with the words:

"Well, chaps."

The day's exercises had already been worked out and they were comparatively simple, for at this stage they were only photographing the bombers and fighter escorts on their way to the target, before any air combats developed.

"Simply a straightforward mass flight today, chaps," Blake said. "Remember the weave and the crossover which we've been practicing? It's going quite well and I'd like to see it today. Flights of nine bombers in three vics each, and four fighters in vic as escorts. We make for the coast and then turn and fly along it toward Málaga."

This was carefully translated into Spanish for the benefit of the pilots. Someone went forward and moved the models around on their sticks while Quentin Lawrence, the air unit director, stood in front of a model of the Psychedelic Monster and tried out his camera angles. He turned to John Hawke and Hawke's American copilot, Duane Egli. He moved the B-25 model around and in between the planes.

"Think you'll be able to cope?" he asked.

Hawke nodded calmly. "We can fly very easily whatever is best for you. We are much faster than the others—we have lots of spare speed and plenty of altitude. I can't do the impossible, of course, but you can talk me into doing practically anything else. We can weave in and out and zoom around quite a bit."

Lawrence said: "You can't fly backward, though, can you?" and grinned.

"No," said Hawke, "but sometimes we can make you feel that's what we're doing."

He wasn't kidding, either.

The two cameramen who would be flying with us had now joined the briefing. Skeets Kelly, a long streak of a man with a face like an Afghan hound, is a gray-haired veteran in his fifties who only seems happy when he has a camera in his hand and his feet are off the ground. Many of the most spectacular climaxes in British films on rooftops, towers, swinging cranes and ships' mastheads have been photographed by him. For the flying sequences in *The Battle of Britain* he would be riding in the tail gunner's position, open to the wind, with nothing to keep him floating off into space during the maneuvers except a safety belt.

His companion, sitting beside him on a three-legged shooting stick, was Johnny Jordan, a specialist in air-to-air camerawork, particularly in helicopters. During the climactic sequence of the Bond film *You Only Live Twice*, when an air battle develops between several helicopters, one came too close to Jordan's craft and a propeller sliced into one of his legs dangling over the side. He took pictures of the all-but-severed limb as the helicopter descended ("It was the only thing I could think of to do") and then spent months in a hospital while the surgeons tried to sew it back together again. It was eventually amputated below the knee, and Jordan was back in air-camera work a few weeks later.

"They offered me a ground job," he said, "but I wasn't having any. I love the work. Anyway, having only one leg can be very convenient in cramped spaces in planes and copters. I just take off my tin substitute and I can crawl into places I could never make before."

The pilots began to break off into groups, bomber pilots chattering to each other in one lot, fighter pilots rather ostentatiously keeping to themselves.

"It never changes," said Hawke wryly, nodding at the bomber boys first and then at the fighter pilots. "The sheep—and the goats."

"What are you," someone asked him, "a hybrid?"

"I'm just a man who drives a bus," Hawke said.

There was a rap of a stick on the blackboard.

"All right, chaps," Blake called out. "Shall we get cracking?"

I walked out of the hangar with Connie Edwards, one of the four pilots from the Confederate air force; he and his companions would be flying Messerschmitts with the formation. The sun had come out, and shone down on the row upon row of Spanish Heinkel bombers, now disguised with German crosses and swastikas.

"D'you realize that's practically the whole of the Spanish bomber force out there?" Edwards said. There was a pause and then he added: "Say, now's the time for Gibraltar to invade Spain, wouldn't you think?"

We had a rendezvous with the bombers and fighters just off the Andalusian coast at a height of ten thousand feet, and while we climbed toward it over the yellow fields of mustard and the cluster of pink and ocher farm buildings, I had a chance to look around the B-25. Once upon a time this plane had flown over the Pacific on missions for the U.S. air force. But now where cannon and machine guns had been, camera positions had been built instead. The whole of the front of the fuselage had been ripped out and replaced by a huge cowl of specially molded plexiglass big enough and clear enough to allow a 65-millimeter wide-screen color camera to shoot through it. The end of the tail had been taken out completely and a camera rigged up in the rear gunner's position. There were places for cameras to shoot through the side windows; and when the bomb bay was opened a camera could be lowered through it capable of shooting over a whole 360-degree field, controlled by a cameraman sitting just above it. For this flight, Jordan was in the nose and Skeets Kelly in the tail, though there would be other cameramen aboard for later flights. On top of the fuselage amidships was a large plexiglass dome under which the air unit director stood, from which he could see the sky around him. A few yards ahead, under another cowl, stood the air traffic controller. All of us were linked together by earphones inside the plane, so that the air unit director could transmit instructions to Hawke and his copilot, the cameraman and the air controller. In addition, the air controller was in direct communication with the Heinkels and Messerschmitts so that he could pass on the air unit director's orders; and, of course, Hawke had his own circuit for communicating with the ground.

The extra refinement which turned this formidably equipped flying camera plane into an airborne studio was a television set built into a position beside the air unit director under the big dome. This was connected to the camera positions inside the plane, so that by looking at the screen the director could see exactly what they were shooting. But not only that. The set was also equipped with videotape, so that after a particular maneuver was completed the director could play it back to make sure that he had got just the formations and angles he wanted.

I was standing in the well of the plane just behind Hawke and his copilot, Duane Egli, and suddenly I saw Egli pointing. The Heinkels in a beautiful succession of vic formations were coming toward us, Messerschmitts weaving over and under them as they approached. The air was all at once filled with the chatter of Spanish voices, like deep-throated birds, over which came Hawke's crisp tones:

"There they are, Quentin, at one-o'clock. What d'you want me to do?"

"Get under them, get under them!" The air unit director sounded very excited. "Let Johnny get a shot of them coming over. Then bank around so's we can get a shot of them from an angle."

"Okay."

Hawke pointed the nose of the B-25 upward and I gripped the side of the plane as we suddenly surged forward, and then we were going straight at them. The chatter of Spanish voices increased in number and decibels as they saw us. One of the planes on the wing wavered a little, as if flinching, and then got back into line again. Just as it looked as if we were going to smash straight into the nose of the middle plane, I saw Hawke push his stick forward and we were underneath them, close enough to scrape their sky blue bellies. I could see Hawke's substantial shoulders shaking with impish laughter at the momentary panic he had caused; and then almost immediately he was banking sharply away himself as a Messerschmitt came hurtling past the tip of our nose.

"That was a beautiful job, amigo. You almost took the paint off 'em."

It was the voice of Connie Edwards. We could see him in his cockpit as he streaked past us, one hand giving us the thumbs-up sign.

And then we were round again, shooting from the side, and then beetling after the Heinkels, catching up and passing them and then staying steadily in the lead, a cable's length ahead.

"Is this where you want me to fly backward, Quentin?" Hawke shouted.

"If only you could!" the director shouted back.

Hawke: "Tell Skeets to get ready!"

Skeets Kelly: "I'm ready for anything!"

Almost at once it was as if someone had trodden hard on the air brakes of a speeding truck. The B-25 seemed to be coming to a grinding halt in midair, and my head was butting into Duane Egli's back. The flaps were down, the engines were cut, the whole plane was all but stalling; and once more, timed and measured with precision, the fleet of Heinkels were roaring over us and there were those familiar sky blue bellies just over our heads, near enough to trim our hair.

An hour later, after a series of loops, banks, rolls and dives ("This crate will do anything you ask of her.") we were back down on the ground and the first session with the bombers was over.

We saw the rushes of that afternoon's work a few days later, in San Sebastian, with Harry Saltzman in the audience and most of the members of the film unit. The planes looked like gorgeous butterflies flitting about the sky. They were almost too pretty to be true.

"What do you think, Harry?" he was asked by Bert Bates, the man who would have the job of editing the film.

"Beautiful!" he replied sourly.

"Too beautiful!" said Hawke. "You see, it isn't as easy as it looks—not even with all this equipment. It takes hard work, painful rehearsal, and when you are ten seconds too early or too late, you miss the big dramatic shot and get pretty pictures instead."

"That's the trouble," said Johnny Jordan. "It ain't like making films on the ground at all."

"No," said Skeets Kelly wryly. "For one thing, there ain't no chalk marks in the sky."

General Adolf Galland flew into Seville on the afternoon of March 23, 1968, to find cameramen and reporters from practically every nation in the West waiting to meet him. With him was Wing Commander Stanford-Tuck, DSO, DFC, who had been one of the most daring pilots in the RAF during the Battle of Britain and had shot down several fighters in Galland's squadrons. It was one of Galland's pilots who, in turn, shot him down. He was then sent to a prisoner-of-war camp from which, for that was the sort of character he was, he made three attempts to escape, the third time successfully. When the war ended, Stanford-Tuck interrogated Galland. From these wartime encounters the two had become friends, and what more natural? In war they had shared the same pursuits and in peacetime they shared the same hobbies; for though Galland was now an entrepreneur and Tuck had become a mushroom farmer, they both continued to be galvanized by the hunting instinct which had made them such successful fighter pilots, and a love of shooting and the chase bound them together. They shot duck and geese together in England and Germany; they stalked chamois together in the Austrian Tyrol; they went to Hungary together to hunt deer and wild boars. It could not have been more appropriate that Galland should be the expert adviser on the German sequences of *The Battle of Britain* and Tuck the technical overseer of the scenes with the RAF.

With their hands clasped and their arms around each other's shoulders, the two ex-enemy friends posed for their pictures and provided the cameramen with an excellent physical contrast: Galland sallow, suave, running slightly to jowls, Tuck very much the outdoor English officer type, his flesh spare upon the cheekbones, his complexion highly colored. I noticed that whenever he could he stepped out of range of both cameras and reporters, and rightly so, for this was Galland's day. For the Spanish press particularly Galland was a hero (a pro-Franco hero, that is). During the Spanish civil war he had been one of the young Luftwaffe pilots sent by Hitler to give aid to General Franco—and also to get a little practice in the art of aerial warfare—and he had cut his teeth as a combat flier by escorting Nazi bombers on their raids against Spanish government forces.

The Spanish reporters and photographers could not have too much of him, and with great amiability he answered every question and adopted every pose they asked of him. When he climbed into the car with his friend to be driven to the Tablada air base, they streamed after him—and almost at once were witnesses of another news-making confrontation. For waiting to greet him there was Commandante Pedro Santa Cruz, and he was an old friend who had never been an enemy, for these two had always fought on the same side. They fell upon each other's necks and embraced.

Santa Cruz had been chosen by the producers of *The Battle of Britain* to fly with and command the pilots of the Messerschmitts to be used in the film, and it was a good choice. He is one of the world's greatest fliers. He flew with Galland during the Spanish civil war, and when Germany attacked the Soviet Union in 1941 he left for Berlin immediately, and though his own country remained neutral he flew Messerschmitts against the Red air force along the Russian front. He too was in appearance a sharp contrast to Galland, who looked like an earthbound businessman beside him. You could almost read Santa Cruz's history in his face. Down his left cheek was a deep scar inflicted in a duel with sabers at Heidelberg in the 1930s. His skin was coffee brown and of the leathery toughness of one who has spent his days seasoning it in the sun and pickling it by night in more convivial places. The eyes were hard, green brown in color, and the lines around them were deep. It was the face of a man who knows what it is like to kill, but is not afraid of being killed; a ruthless face, until it broke into a huge smile of delight at the sight of Galland.

"Amigo, amigo!"

They slapped each other's shoulders, they stamped

their feet, they jabbered at each other in a mixture of Spanish and German. And then, tailed by the delighted cameramen, still arm in arm, they marched off toward the Messerschmitts. Soon they were climbing in and out of them, fondling them as if they were beautiful women.

"How long since you flew one of these, Dolfo?" asked Santa Cruz.

"Twenty-six years," said Galland.

The Spaniard pointed to the two-seater Messerschmitt at the end of the line.

"Let's see what you can do after all that time, amigo," he said. "Come up with me. This one has dual controls."

For just a moment I saw Galland hesitate, and then he nodded quickly.

"I'll need some overalls," he said.

For the second time in one day, those of us on the Tablada air base saw an exhibition of flying to take our breath away. It was Santa Cruz who took the Messerschmitt off the ground but it was plainly Adolf Galland who was in control a few minutes later. At first he was high in the sky, banking, looping, trying the plane out for size, getting the feel, and then suddenly, as if the warm-up was over and the real game was beginning, the plane began to dive. About a mile away it leveled off and then came like a bullet toward us, the height of a house to begin with, but then lower and lower and lower, until he was practically shaving the grass.

"Who needs a lawn mower with Dolfo around," Stanford-Tuck said quietly. And then he added: "There's only one thing he hasn't done yet, but I think he'll do it before he comes down."

And Galland did. He pulled the plane up to about fifty feet and set his sights on the airfield, and then, just when he was over our heads, we saw one wing coming down. We held our breaths. Seconds later the Messerschmitt was turning over, upside down and then over again, so close to the ground that we thought he was going to scrape it. Then he was away again up into the sky.

"That," said Stanford-Tuck, "is the famous Galland roll. He used to do that every time he shot down a British plane during the Battle of Britain."

Five minutes later Galland, followed by a jubilant Santa Cruz, was walking back toward us.

"You wouldn't think he was fifty-six, would you?" said Stanford-Tuck fondly.

But when Galland reached us, I noticed that the back and front of his overalls were wringing wet. The sweat which must have poured out of him during the flight had gone right through his suit.

As It Was in 1940

Though Göring had decided to call off the attacks on Britain's radar stations he did not relax his relentless strafing and bombing of the RAF forward airfields. He did not appear to be fully aware of it, but this was having devastating results.

Most of the RAF's forward airfields had temporarily been put out of action. Dozens of planes had been destroyed by fire on the ground. Air Vice Marshal Keith Park, commanding 11 Group, was desperate. He had made an arrangement with his commander-in-chief, Sir Hugh Dowding, that whenever he was in dire need of help he could call upon the aid of the fighter planes of 12 Group, to the north. It had been made plain that once he SOS'd for help, they would make his needs their first priority and fly in.

What he needed them for was to protect his airfields from marauding Nazi bombers while his own squadrons fought Galland and his fellow Luftwaffe fighter pilots overhead. Unfortunately, the commander of 12 Group, Air Vice Marshal Leigh-Mallory, and his pilots chose to consider this a menial role in the great battle. They wanted to be in there fighting, too. In fact, there had already been charges from 11 Group that fighter planes from 12 Group were straying into their area, creating confusion among their flight controllers on the ground, and "poaching" on the 11 Group preserves by attacking German aircraft which should have been left to them. One of those involved in these incidents was Douglas Bader, who commanded a wing in 12 Group, and led an attack over what was said to be 11 Group territory during which seven German aircraft were shot down.

Keith Park complained to Dowding and to Leigh-Mallory. It became clear subsequently that what he was complaining about was not so much the incursions of a neighboring group's fighters over his area, as to their independence from his control—for he needed to utilize them where they could be most useful to his overall defensive plan.

Bader flew back to his base at Duxford, in Cambridgeshire, to find that a complaint had been lodged against him.

"It was absolute coals, old boy, to suggest I was out of line," Bader said.* "Look, it's no good saying to you when you go up, there's that line Maidstone-Canterbury-Maidstone, and you mustn't go over that. I mean, if you're flying at twenty thousand feet you can be fifteen or twenty miles beyond that and it's still only just under your wing. After all, you've got to remember that twenty-eight years ago we were young chaps and we were trying to destroy enemy aircraft. Well, if the aircraft were over Ashford instead of Canterbury, you can't say, 'Well, I can't go over there.' You go and shoot 'em down anyway. When we got back and heard about the complaint, well, it was a bloody good laugh. No one would have shot them down if we hadn't. It was over the lunch

---

* In a conversation with Peter Townsend at Duxford in July 1968.

period. 11 Group weren't up. I wasn't annoyed at the accusations. I just laughed."

Obviously, it was a mistake for Keith Park to complain about "poaching." But he was suspicious of Leigh-Mallory's intentions toward him (quite rightly, as it turned out) and he lashed out too soon. He had stronger grounds for his complaints toward the end of August. By this time the Luftwaffe attacks on his forward airfields were so damaging that Manston was a pitted desert of chalk dust and had to be evacuated, and many another base was almost permanently out of action.

On August 27, 1940, Park sent an SOS to 12 Group. His planes were up fighting strong Luftwaffe attacks all over Kent and the Thames estuary. His airfields were once more in dire peril from German fighters and bombers. He asked Leigh-Mallory to protect them, to send his fighters at once.

They did not come. 12 Group was "otherwise engaged."

VI

"A Nazi Salute? Never, Never, Never !"

DURING THE WEEK ended March 24, 1968, *The Battle of Britain* spent $348,000, and there were no signs that it would cost them less during each of the sixteen weeks to come. The film was one day ahead of schedule, but this was due more to the adaptability of Guy Hamilton and the speed and efficiency of the unit than to the weather. Before the film had begun, there had been many conferences to decide what sort of weather conditions the actual Battle of Britain had been fought under, and if the film should try to imitate them exactly. It had been agreed, after some study and much argument that, though July–September 1940 was not quite as blue and gold as some middle-aged people chose to remember it, there had been quite a lot of sunshine—and it had been decided that sunny skies should be shown in the film.

It was for this reason that the first and second units had come to Spain for their ground scenes, in order to benefit from the early spring in the south. (The air unit *had* come, of course, since the Spanish air force would hardly have consented to the removal of its Heinkels from the country.) But Spain had let them down. Not only had there been quite a lot of rain, but even on fine days the sun had taken hours to break through so that the unit, on set at 8:00 a.m. and set up, would have to wait around until 11:00 or even 12:00; added to which, cloud formations would roll in and obscure the sun again for half an hour or an hour at a time.

During these periods it was interesting to watch the reactions of the director and the producer. Guy Hamilton would pace up and down, hands behind his back, head and body thrust forward at an angle, a canvas sun hat crammed on his head, face blank with misery, a very sad Monsieur Hulot indeed. Benny Fisz would be circulating among the unit, clasping everyone around the shoulders, insisting, "Don't worry, dear boy, it will be wonderfully sunny this afternoon," smiling at all and sundry, and all the time eating his heart out with despair.

In the meantime, Freddie Young, the cameraman, would be chatting to his assistants and reminiscing about old times, but every so often lifting his face and his dark lens to the sky. He was the one you had to watch, and through all his misery Guy Hamilton never ceased to be aware of him. For he would suddenly say:

"You ready, Guy?"

Immediately he would be at Young's side, and all the unit would be watching. Young would stare at the sky again.

"In five minutes," he would say. "We'll get about three minutes sunshine, I think. Is that enough for you?"

"Yes."

107

Derek Cracknell, the assistant, would lift the bull-horn.

"All right, fellas. Places now. We've got three minutes' sunshine, Freddie says. So let's not waste it. If anybody does, they get it right up the butt."

Milch, Fink and a group of German pilots would be lined up and waiting. Then everyone would grow still, watching Freddie Young staring skyward through his lens, his gentle nut brown face expectant.

It would still be cloudy when he would turn and say:

"Okay, Guy."

Guy Hamilton would nod to the clapper boy. Cracknell would call for background action behind the principal plays. Hamilton would cry:

"All right. Action! *Los!*"

And just as the cameras started turning, the sun would break through. The words would be said, the motions gone through. Cut. Then:

"That was fine. But let's do it just once more." A turn of Hamilton's head to Karl Fox-Dürring, who was liaising between the director and the German players: "Karl, could you ask Herr Harnisch if he could loosen up a little? He moves as if he's got a poker stuck up his back."

Harnisch (suavely in English): "Give me a moment, Mr. Hamilton, and I'll unlimber myself."

He made as if to take an invisible ramrod from under his Luftwaffe jacket, and everyone laughed, including Hamilton.

"Right. Once more. Action. *Los!*"

The sun went in just as the director called "Cut" once again. Two takes in a little under three minutes, and a very smooth one the second time.

Ben Fisz was beaming happily. Even though the

film was costing $240 a minute, it would not seem too much if it always went like this.

After one hard day of long waits and sudden spurts of activity, I went back to the Florida Apartments, in downtown Seville, with Freddie Young to join him and his wife for dinner. On the way we stopped off at a local cinema to see the latest rushes which had just come in from London, with Guy Hamilton and Bert Bates, the editor, as the only other members of the audience. There were some more shots of the Heinkels and Messerschmitts weaving serenely across the cloud-flecked sky, and these were watched in a heavy silence.

The rest of the rushes were devoted to a sequence shot three days before of the Heinkels coming out of their pens on the airfield, taxiing across the field, and taking off against a dawn sky toward London. I recognized Freddie Young's work at once. In terms of present-day bombers, the Heinkels were puny planes and yet, for the purpose of this scene, they must be made to seem huge, lumbering, loaded with menace. Young's achievement was to have given them these very qualities and endowed them with an ugly beauty that chilled you as you watched them. He had scaled down his colors and filled the sky behind the bombers with a suffusion of sun-tinged clouds, and as I sat there I was back in the days of World War II.

"Not bad at all," said Hamilton as we went our different ways.

Freddie Young has been in the film business since he left school at fifteen. In 1967 he celebrated his fiftieth anniversary as a cameraman and practically every star, director and producer within flying distance, from Elsie Randolph to Ava Gardner, from Peter O'Toole to Sean Connery, from Herbert Wilcox to David Lean, from Sam Speigel to Harry Saltzman, came to wish him well. He has worked with most of the great stars and nearly all the great directors and there are few who don't love him, for he is an artist, a master craftsman, and a very gentle man.

His wife Joan was waiting for us with whisky-sodas and a home-cooked English dinner. The age difference between Young and his wife is vast, but there is little doubt about the depth of the affection they feel for each other. They met in Thailand and Hong Kong while Young was filming *Lord Jim*. His wife of many years had recently died painfully of cancer; Joan was working as an assistant cutter on the film; and propinquity soon ripened into something much warmer. They were married during the film, and their son was born a year later here in Seville, where Young was then making *Doctor Zhivago* with David Lean. We took our glasses and went into the bedroom to look at the moppet; he was fast asleep with a look of an affectionate imp on his tiny sunburned face. The expression on the two Youngs as they looked down on him was wonderful to behold.

It is not simply because he was working on one of his films when David was born that Freddie Young worships David Lean. In his opinion, he is the greatest director in the history of the cinema. Over dinner we talked of Young's many films, but he always kept coming back to *Lawrence of Arabia* and *Doctor Zhivago*, Lean's films on which he won his two Oscars.

"A strange man, David," he said. "He'll brood for hours over a scene while everyone hangs around, waiting on his inspiration. Then suddenly he is ready

110

to go and wants to know why the crew isn't all set up. So I learned to keep my crew on the alert and, very discreetly, we would edge up the camera and the lights as he moved around and thought up his scene and the angles. Then, when he swung around and said, 'We'll do it this way,' I was ready for him. 'You bastard, Freddie,' he'd cry. 'You've been following me.'"

We talked of the problems of *The Battle of Britain* and of the fantastic difficulties in the way of re-creating the vast scope of it, on the ground and in the air.

"Do you know," he said, "this film is going to have less fake in it than any I can remember. Of course we'll have scenes in the studios with actors in the cockpits and all that. But most of it will be done in the actual planes. Not that I'm against faking," he added, quickly; "if it's well done it can be better than the real thing. Take the desert scenes in *Lawrence*. All right, we went to Jordan, but some of the best scenes were shot at Almería here in Spain. Take *Zhivago*. We sent a second unit all the way to Finland to get the big snow scenes, but we scrapped most of them. They wanted me to do them, and as we were shooting here in Spain again, I took the unit right up into the Estremadura mountains in midwinter. The only trouble was that when the snow fell it wouldn't stick. So you know what we did?" He chuckled. "We found this big marble quarry and we bought all their marble dust off them. We spread it inches deep over acres of ground. It was marvelous! Sparkled just the right way when the sun caught it. Then we put soap over flat parts of it—this was the lake sequence—so that when the cavalry marched over it the horses skidded as if they were on ice."

Joan added hurriedly: "They weren't hurt if they fell, you see. The ground underneath was soft."

I asked him what he thought of Guy Hamilton as a director to work with, and I could almost hear him comparing him with David Lean.

"A craftsman," he said. "He knows just what he wants and he's not satisfied until he gets it. That means we're going to have tough times on this film before we've finished. There's one thing about Guy. I don't think he likes film stars."

"He has a point," said Joan.

It would very soon be Easter, and no one in Seville wants a film company around at that time of the year. The religious processions take place. The bullfights are on. The visitors flow in from all parts of the world. Who needs actors? The flying unit would naturally stay on and billet on the airfield if necessary, but it was time for the main unit to go.

When I got back to the Luz Hotel, where most of the actors and crews were staying, the usual call sheet for next day was missing from the board beside the porter's desk, and instead there was a notice:

FIRST UNIT—ALL DEPARTMENTS

Tuesday, March 26, 1968

NO SHOOTING CALL FIRST UNIT (Packing-Up Day)
UNIT LEAVES HOTELS AT 8:00 A.M. ALL DEPARTMENT HEADS TO SUPERVISE THE PACKING OF EQUIPMENT ON THE LORRIES DUE TO LEAVE FOR SAN SEBASTIÁN BY NOON.
A.M./LUNCH/P.M. MEAL BREAKS WILL BE SERVED AT THE CATERING TENT.

SOUND UNIT TO RECORD WILD EFFECTS TRACKS AS AGREED.

CATERING TO PACK AND PREPARE FOR MOVE TO SAN SEBASTIAN.

CHAPMAN CRANE TO LEAVE A.M. FOR SAN SEBASTIÁN BY ROAD.

PERSONAL LUGGAGE LABELS ARE AVAILABLE FROM THE PRODUCTION OFFICE.

WILL ALL PERSONNEL SEE THAT EQUIPMENT AND LUGGAGE ARE CORRECTLY LABELED?

THE CHARTER PLANE WILL LEAVE ON THURS-DAY IN THE EARLY MORNING FOR SAN SEBASTIÁN.

THE PRODUCTION AND HOTEL ADDRESS IN SAN SEBASTIÁN IS:

> Hotel María Cristina
> Paseo de la Zurriola
> Telephone: San Sebastián 3071

The message was unsigned, but it was plainly the work of Claud Hudson, the unit production manager, an expert on location work whose boast it was that he had never lost a bag or a member of a unit yet. He was also the man who made sure that there was caviar and champagne en route.

Upstairs in Derek Coyte's suite a party was, as usual, in progress, only a little more hectic on this occasion since it could reasonably be called a farewell party. Two extremely attractive secretaries from the publicity department—both wearing the startlingly short miniskirts which by now were the talk of Seville—were circulating drinks to a motley gang of actors, technicians, writers and cameramen. Colonel Connie Edwards of the Confederates was sitting on the floor, playing his guitar and singing, and every time one of the girls passed him she dropped down on her pretty knees and fed him a mouthful from his glass of brandy.

Coyte used to be the quietly successful head of publicity at the Rank Studios at Pinewood, in England, until Harry Saltzman asked him to join him and organize the publicity for *The Battle of Britain*. He immediately asked (and got) the salary and budget he needed, and blossomed. He even impressed his tough American rivals at United Artists when he arrived to address a luncheon meeting of UA representatives from all over America, most of whom had never heard of the Battle of Britain.

"Keep your speech short, make it simple, and sell 'em, boy," he was told.

He rose and said:

"Gentlemen, I am not going to make a speech about *The Battle of Britain*. I think it should be allowed to speak for itself."

He then turned up a tape recording he had had made before leaving England which brought in the thud of bombs and the whine of engines, the jokes of bombed Londoners, and the voice of Churchill telling the world that Britons would fight in the air and on the beaches. It was a small gem of compilation, and plenty of the listeners were in tears by the time it was finished.

Coyte, a big broad man in his forties, with thick-lensed spectacles, an owlish face and a laugh which boils out of him like steam from a kettle, has a large capacity for food, drink and people. He had been on the go, with little time for sleep, for a long time now but his galvanic energy showed no sign of flagging.

"Señor!" he cried in greeting as I entered the room (he had been calling people "señor" long before he came to Spain). "Help yourself to a drink. I was just

saying that this film has three imponderables—the
weather, the planes and the stars. When the weather
is bad the planes can't fly, and when the planes can't
fly the shooting schedule has to be altered, and when
the shooting schedule has to be altered the stars of
the picture can't make their dates. Imponderables! It's
terrible!" He boiled with laughter. "That's why I can't
tell you who are going to be the big stars of this film.
I just can't tell you! Because of the . . ."

"Imponderables!" everyone shouted gaily.

He nodded. "So what can I do to keep all you nice
people happy while we wait on the weather?"

"You can fill me with another drink," said the dark
girl in the leather skirt from the *Daily Mail*.

"And," said the amiable man from *Life* magazine,
"we will all get up at dawn, in spite of our hangovers,
and write nice pieces about the battle for our papers."

He was quite right. These were early days in the
film, but there were TV units from CBS, BBC, French
and German TV, and reporters and cameramen from
Life, Paris-Match, Quick, Der Stern, Oggi, Up and
half a dozen British and American newspapers on the
spot already. The premiere of *The Battle of Britain*
was eighteen months away, but in the next week or
two there would be pieces about the film from all
parts of the world.

I made my way over to a corner of the room where
a group was surrounding a large, fleshy-faced man
with long sideboards and great protuberant eyes like
blue humbugs, which seemed about to start out
of his face when he laughed. This was Andrew
Campbell, a gifted eccentric from the art department
whose job it was to draw sequences, like a series of
comic strips, of particular scenes in the film so that
the art director could build his sets and the film direc-

tor could place and move his actors. He seemed to be talking about the difficulties of getting air battles on the screen (he had been choreographing some of the maneuvers himself).

"The trouble is," he was saying, "that even the most obvious scene is open to so many interpretations. You say that a plane should fly into camera at the top left hand of the screen to the lower-right-hand corner, but the way in which it can move from A to B, the way it postures, the way it behaves inside the frame can be tremendously complicated. I've been trying to get a common point of agreement about this." He didn't mention any names, but the inference was that he had been trying to get it from the last air unit director and the overall director of the film, Guy Hamilton. "I've tried to visualize the movements in my drawings, but it can be a disappointing exercise because the director looks at my sequence of events and then takes a scene right out of context, and then juxtaposes it with another scene which has nothing whatever to do with my sequence."

Campbell made a comically exaggerated grimace of disgust at this enormity.

"The swine, the cad!" said someone.

"Agreed, dear boy," Campbell went on. "You build a mosaic and the director decides quite arbitrarily to put in a different piece of mosaic and color. Crackle, crackle, it breaks one's heart. And yet if they only follow one's line of thought and vision, it can work." He looked up at me. "You, sir! Did you see that awful James Bond film, *You Only Live Twice?* You did? I am ashamed for you, sir. But on the other hand, there was one sequence in that film of remarkable interest visually. The one with the helicopters—the one where the small spaceship is encapsulated by the big space-ship. Now this was planned most meticulously before-hand in sketch form. The director had a lot to do with it, but the drawings were very interesting and it worked very well. You could see the inexorable progressive development. And that, children, is what we need to see in this film—inexorable progressive development!"

One of the miniskirts came up, bussed him gently on his sweaty nose with great affection and said: "Oh, Andrew, you're using those words again!"

He looked after her green-clad thighs and sighed. "An interesting medium," he said. "Although there are novelists who embark on a book without a master plan, I would find it hard to believe that generally speaking they don't have one in their mind. But this medium—the fascinating thing is not so much what it says but the way that it says it. That is why the classic example of people like Clouzot coming into the commercial cinema is marvelous, because they know how to put a rather mundane action on the screen and yet invest it with a very arresting mood of significance. It may derive from the choice of a lens, the way in which the camera tracks, any other slender factor, but they make this tremendous difference. Hitchcock can make a man walking into a room intriguing. It's the difference perhaps between Praxiteles and the student at the Croydon School of Art."

He bugged his eyes out at us and held out his glass.

"Am I talking too much?" he asked. A pause and then: "This film, now. If only we had a director who could make the *planes* talk and the actors *fly*. Now *that* would be a sequence worth drawing."

While the unit was moving to San Sebastián I

117

made my own way by car via Madrid, and the splendors of the Prado. The weather was poor and it got worse as we traveled north. Somewhere in the Basque country, in a mountain mist, I passed the huge Chapman crane grinding its way over a tortuous stretch of atrocious road. The crew waved to me cheerfully.

It turned out that though San Sebastián was the headquarters of the unit, the first scenes were going to be shot at a small railway station called Irurzun, sixty miles away on the main line to Pamplona. Weatherwise, a worse place could hardly have been chosen because the surrounding mountains not only brought in mist and rain but also got in the way of the camera. The important sequence to be shot at Irurzun was known in the script as Göring's Train Sequence and deals with the arrival and subsequent departure of Field Marshal Göring. He has been on a tour of the German fighter stations in the Pas de Calais. There are definitely *no* mountains in that part of France.

On the other hand, the unit had no option. This was the only railway station the Spanish authorities were prepared to make available, and even so normal traffic must be allowed to continue. Every time a train whistled through or stopped to let down passengers, shooting had to be suspended; and though at first the unit got a kick out of the expression on the passengers' faces as they descended (for they found French advertisements, German swastikas, and Franco-German signs plastered all over the Spanish ones), this became an irritation after a time, especially when a shot was interrupted during the only good weather of the morning.

The art department under Maurice Carter's direction had done a remarkable job with Göring's train.

Only one side of it would be seen in camera, but that side had been meticulously copied from photographs and drawings of the original, and built onto a Spanish dining coach. On each side of the saloon were flak guns mounted on flatcars and manned by Spanish extras in German uniforms. A Spanish engine driver drove the train into and out of the station, with a Spanish-speaking assistant carrying a walkie-talkie standing beside him to tell him when to stop and start.

Providing the coordination was right, the scenes with and on Göring's train were comparatively simple, but they were also vitally important. I had better explain why so that the subsequent row between Guy Hamilton and General Adolf Galland can be better understood.

The sequence takes place at a vital moment both in the film and in the history of the Battle of Britain. The blitz on London has begun and wave upon wave of bombers are pounding the city every day. It can't be long before the escorting German fighters have wiped out the RAF defenders and can bomb at will, stunning and terrifying the populace before invading them. When Göring arrives at the Pas de Calais he is still confident that this will be achieved. Like many another Nazi leader, he believes his own propaganda, and according to the figures they are putting out, the RAF is all but wiped out. But in the course of his tour he learns the truth. The bombers are being shot down in large numbers. Why? For two reasons. The Messerschmitts escorting them haven't enough fuel to accompany them to London and still fight the Spitfires of the RAF. In any case, they have discovered that a Spitfire is a better plane than the Me-109. It can fly faster, it can turn more tightly, it can outmaneuver.

119

In the face of the disastrous losses which have begun to hit the Luftwaffe, Fink, the bomber commander, and Osterkamp, chief of staff to Kesselring (commander of the Second Airfleet) have started to quarrel among themselves. Kesselring ineffectually tries to soothe them. Göring is furious both at the news of the situation and the low morale of his commanders. There is a meeting at the fighter base in France from which Galland's squadron (he is called Falke in the film) flies out against the RAF. Falke and his fellow flier, Foehn, stand by while Göring flares out at Fink and Osterkamp:

480. New Angle. Conference. Göring paces up and down.

GÖRING
I see it very clearly, my friends. You are spoiled.

FINK
Our losses might be reduced if our formations were more closely escorted by fighters, sir.

OSTERKAMP (quietly)
The fighters are always there.

GÖRING (looking at FINK)
But not closely enough. Is that it?

OSTERKAMP
You yourself were a fighter pilot. The fighter is a hunter.

GÖRING
I was a fighter pilot. I was not a coward.

KESSELRING
There is no suggestion of cowardice.

GÖRING (louder)
I am making the suggestion! From now on the fighters *will* stay closer to our bombers.

OSTERKAMP

And lose their natural advantages of surprise, speed
and . . .

GÖRING (flares)

You will follow orders! . . . The invasion cannot
start until we have cleared the skies.

There is silence as GÖRING stalks up and down. He suddenly stops, turns toward the young fighter pilots, FOEHN
and FALKE, and beams at them.

GÖRING (tone changes)

Now come, my friends. I have chastised you. But I
am here to help. You, Foehn—anything you want?

FOEHN remains silent.

GÖRING

Falke?

FALKE

A squadron of Spitfires.

GÖRING is furious. He walks away.

It is from this merry little encounter that Göring returns to the station to board his train, and his wrath
has not simmered down when it is time to go. The
usual roster of generals and other high officers of the
Luftwaffe are assembled to bid him farewell. Osterkamp and Kesselring are in front. He harangues them
fiercely. Hitler demands the destruction of the RAF,
he shouts at them, and what Hitler demands Hitler
must have. *So annihilate the RAF or else* . . . after
which the train draws away and the Luftwaffe officers
raise their hands in abashed salute.

Now it so happens that at least during the period of
the Battle of Britain it was never the custom of the
officers of the Luftwaffe to give the Nazi salute (or
German "*Gruss*") except when they were personally

greeting Adolf Hitler. To salute anyone else they always brought the fingers of their right hand to the peak of their caps, like officers in any civilized country. Luftwaffe veterans are very insistent about this; they were flying for Germany and not for a political ideology, which a Hitler salute might indicate; it is an article of faith with them, particularly today.

Now Guy Hamilton had so far shown absolutely no deviation from this code of behavior in the German scenes for *The Battle of Britain*. When Luftwaffe officers met each other, when other ranks greeted their superiors, and when Göring arrived in France on his tour of inspection, they were always correctly shown as being given the ordinary military salute. No one raised his hand high in an unspoken "Heil Hitler!"

Until March 29, that is.

On that day General Galland arrived in San Sebastián and we heard that he was being driven out at once to Irurzun. It was reported that he was in a lively mood. He had piloted his own plane from Germany and brought his old commander with him, the real General Osterkamp, and he was out to enjoy himself. This was "his" country, for it was from the San Sebastián front that he had flown out on ground-strafing raids against the Republicans during the Spanish civil war, when General Franco's headquarters were in nearby Burgos.

In the two days preceding Galland's arrival, the unit had managed to film Göring's arrival, but not without some difficulty. The Chapman crane had broken down on the last lap and had arrived late. The weather had turned cloudy and cold. There had been several interruptions from passing trains and gawping passengers. And in addition, there had been a slight passage at arms between Guy Hamilton and a charming, gray-haired, sixtyish ex-German officer named Colonel Brustellin who was acting as unit technical expert (Galland was overall adviser) on this particular scene, which called for the train to come to a halt before the reception committee and for a Luftwaffe soldier to climb down first with Göring's personal banner, before the field marshal himself descended from the train.

Hamilton had not been too satisfied with this.

"That Luftwaffe uniform is too bloody dull," he said. "We need some color." He turned to the assistant, Derek Cracknell. "Go and ask Brustellin whether it is possible for an SS officer to hold Göring's standard instead."

Brustellin hurried over at once. He was liked by everyone and had tried his best to be helpful, but now he was the Luftwaffe. The peacocks of the SS didn't come into it. It must be a Luftwaffe man, drab uniform or not. He looked very abashed about it. Hamilton on the other hand looked extremely annoyed, but accepted his advice.

Early on March 29, when I arrived at Irurzun, they had just completed a rehearsal of the farewell scene during which Göring shouts at Osterkamp and Kesselring through the window of his train. The train drew away and the two Luftwaffe officers looked up at their master and saluted. It was obvious from the flat look on Hamilton's face that he was dissatisfied, that the scene lacked bite. You could almost hear the wheels of his mind turning over as he searched for a means of getting a wallop into it. Later, in the tent at lunchtime, I began to see the direction in which his mind was going.

"Kesselring was a Nazi, wasn't he?" he asked.

Kesselring had indeed been a member of the Nazi party during his service with the German armed forces. He had been seconded to the Luftwaffe from the army by Hitler for the very reason that he was a trusted member of the party.

"So when Göring screams his head off at them," Hamilton went on, "and when he threatens them with Hitler's anger, why shouldn't I try to show that in the scene? They've all been giving ordinary salutes so far. But in this scene Kesselring reverts to what he is—a Nazi. The others salute. He gives the German 'Gruss.' Hell, there must have been *some* Nazis in the Luftwaffe, and this will symbolize it."

Freddie Young said:

"Are you going to try it out on Brustellin?"

"Hell no!" said Hamilton. "I'm just going to do it!"

About three o'clock in the afternoon, General Galland and General Osterkamp arrived.

The actor who was playing the part of Reichsmarschall Herman Göring was a German actor named Hein Riess. He was a huge man cast almost exactly in the same physical mold as Göring, and not unlike him in face and manner. Normally he was a music-hall singer in Hamburg (one of his better-known appearances had been in a musical called *Wiederholen nach St. Pauli*) but it was in no music-hall spirit that he was approaching this role. He had stipulated that he would accept the part only if Göring was taken seriously and not made a figure of mockery.

In uniform he looked so real that anyone who had met Göring gasped with astonishment. The dress chosen for this occasion was sky blue in color, his chest was covered with medals (Göring's love of gaudy

uniforms was well known) and he carried a gold
Reichsmarschall's baton. As Hein Riess strutted up
and down between takes, heaving with laughter, slap-
ping people on the back, the effect was uncanny.

The farewell scene was rehearsed once again
immediately after the lunch break, but this time as
the train drew away and the officers saluted, Kesselring lifted his hand high in a "Heil Hitler!" There was
no doubt of its effectiveness. It transformed the whole
scene and jolted you back into remembering that here
was a Nazi regime. Brustellin watched it morosely,
but had already realized that his protests were in
vain; and one guessed that he was not unsympathetic
to the symbolism that Hamilton had in mind.

We had been waiting for the weather, and only a
few minutes after Galland and Osterkamp arrived the
skies showed signs of clearing. So greetings were
brief.

"Places, everybody!" Derek Cracknell called.

Hamilton and Freddie Young were up with the
camera crew on the roof of a wagon, looking down on
Göring poised at the window and Osterkamp and
Kesselring staring up at him from the track. Galland
and the real Osterkamp, a fragile little man with a
goatee beard, stood beside me just by the truck.

"You ready, Freddie?"

Young nodded. The clapper boy came forward. The
sound man, Gordon Everett, announced that his tape
was running. Hamilton called out:

"Right. Action! *Los!*"

A few seconds before, the man in the train had
been a fatty named Hein Riess, but now he was suddenly Göring. His face curdled. He was angry. He
leaned forward, waving his baton, and threatened
them with Hitler's wrath.

"You have let me down! You have betrayed me!" he cried.

The train began to pull out of the station, Göring still gesticulating furiously. All the other officers stared up at him, and then lifted their hands to their caps in salute. And then Kesselring, after a brief hesitation, lifted his own hand—in the Nazi greeting.

At which there was a stirring beside me. Suddenly Adolf Galland was running forward, waving his hands. A moment later he was among the actors, shouting angrily:

"No, no, no! A Hitler salute? Never, never, never!"

The actors milled in confusion. I could hear Hamilton crying:

"Cut, cut! Damn, damn, damn! He's ruined my scene. Get that man off my set!"

Galland had come storming back.

"If that scene stays in, I leave the film! You understand?" he cried, belligerently. "I finish!"

Ben Fisz led him away, talking soothingly.

"Don't get so worked up, Dolfo," I could hear him saying.

Guy Hamilton was still looking angry too. He called a break for tea and stalked off to his caravan, after one rancorous look at Galland. General Osterkamp teetered on his tiny feet and tugged his beard, and looked as if he didn't know what it was all about.

Next morning Galland flew back to Germany. He had not changed his mind. He left threatening dire consequences for the film if the scene stayed in.

Guy Hamilton was determined that it should.

As It Was in 1940

The crucial phase of the Battle of Britain had begun on August 24. Göring's visit to his front-line airfields and his angry charges against his commanders and pilots was paying off in an increased aggressiveness on the part of the Luftwaffe. The Reichsmarschall had sent an order to his air fleets bidding them "continue the fight against the enemy until further notice, with the aim of weakening the British fighter forces. The enemy is to be forced to use his fighters by means of ceaseless attacks. In addition, the aircraft industry and the ground organization of the air force are to be attacked . . . by night and day."

The Germans were growing more cunning, too. They were learning how to trick and confuse the radar stations along the south coast of England. Formations of planes would go up in France throughout the day and fly up and down, just within range of the British radar screens. The plotters would guess that a raid was coming and order the defensive fighters to be scrambled, only to discover, once the RAF was airborne, that it was just a bluff.

When they struck now, the Luftwaffe struck hard —at Keith Park's airfields and his reserve fighters, at his complicated and vital communication system, at the aircraft factories and at the oil tanks which provided him with his fuel and kept the wheels of British industry turning.

It was a period when Britain's outlook seemed dire. Dowding was as near to despair as that cold and tireless character could ever come. He was well aware that a great row was boiling up between his front-line commander, Keith Park, and the ambitious Leigh-Mallory to the rear. Which one was right in the tactics they were advocating? For Keith Park was advocating purely defensive tactics. "I am not asking you to shoot down Me-109s," he told his Spitfire pilots, "but to draw them away from the Heinkels and Junkers, leaving them for the Hurricanes to deal with."

To Leigh-Mallory this was too passive altogether. He longed to send his fighters up, in a great wing, to hunt out the Me-109s and blast them out of the skies. So when Keith Park sent his first SOS for help on August 24—at a moment when five hundred bombers were blowing North Weald air base to blazes—it was a big wing that Leigh-Mallory sent from his own base at Duxford, and it took so long to assemble that it arrived too late to save North Weald from destruction.

And, as has been seen, when Park asked again for help on April 27, Leigh-Mallory did not come at all.

It was a black moment. Quarreling commanders, exhausted pilots, unusable airfields and plummeting morale. Could Britain possibly hold out? Would Göring fulfill his promise to Hitler and wipe out the RAF by mid-September—and open the way for a Nazi invasion of Britain?

It was in this critical hour that the Germans once more made a mistake. This time it was fatal.

VII
How to Be
a Director

———◆———

FOR THE MOMENT there were no repercussions from Galland's outburst—although everyone realized that there would be—and Guy Hamilton carried on as if the incident had never happened. Or tried to. The scene was gone through once more, *with* the Nazi salute included, and sent off to London. But after that the weather changed from mediocre to atrocious and the unit sat around in the rain for hour after hour, day after day, waiting for a break in the clouds which would enable them to snatch the final train-sequence shots before the Spanish government claimed back its train and its station. One day it even snowed, carpeting the surrounding hills with a white coating which Freddie Young could not keep out of his picture whatever lenses he used. On that day, of course, the sun came out, but the landscape could hardly be made to look like northern France in September.

"Paddy," shouted Derek Cracknell, "I want you to take a volunteer team and brush that mountain clear

129

of snow." He pointed to a peak in the immediate fore-ground.

Paddy, the propman, was rounding up a team and arming them with brushes before he realized he was being kidded.

To add to the director's worries, the weather news from Seville, where the air unit was still operating, was equally bad. Hamilton was in overall charge of everything which happened on the film, and it was a wearing experience to emerge from a fruitless day in the Basque mountains to hear from the south that there had been no action and no flying there either. He was only too aware of the fact that though the Spanish government had been magnanimous in its loan of the Heinkels for the film, that loan had its time limits and now the days were running out. The vital shots of the bomber formations must be got into the camera before the planes were washed clean of their swastikas and handed back to their owners.

Hamilton's worries were not eased by news from Seville that, like his friend Galland, Santa Cruz, the Messerschmitt leader, was running a temperament.

During one of the maneuvers, it appeared, a Messerschmitt piloted by one of his Spanish fliers had run into trouble when coming into land. Santa Cruz was on the ground that day and he and one of the British air advisers for the film went out on to the strip as the Messerschmitt came over. There was something wrong with its undercarriage, and only one wheel would come down. Nor could the pilot get the single wheel up again when he tried. In the end, he indicated that he was going to come in on one wheel. He did so—a superb landing which brought the Me-109 down on to its wing only at the last minute and did only superficial damage.

Santa Cruz now complained that the British adviser, far from congratulating the pilot on his lucky escape and magnificent airmanship, had rated him for risking damage to one of the company's precious planes. He was now refusing to speak directly to the Englishman and all communications were being made through intermediaries. It was hardly speeding up the action.

As if to make his mood even more morose, news had reached Hamilton that United Artists in New York were worried about the state of the budget on the film. To accountants thousands of miles away it did not matter whether it was raining or not—they wanted to see a daily quota of film go into the can. They had a point, of course; it must be hard to have to pay out $50,000 a day to men who were standing around all day doing absolutely nothing. United Artists were demanding that the Spanish locations should be finished without any further delay and the company brought back to England.

Harry Saltzman was therefore on his way to Spain for urgent conferences with Hamilton and Fisz over the Easter weekend.

"That is one of the terrible things about directing," Hamilton said. We were sitting on a wooden bench in the food tent, eating cheese with red wine and listening to the castanet clatter of the rain on the canvas. "Ninety percent of it isn't filming at all, but doing all the guff. Dealing with producers, for one thing. For instance, Harry Saltzman will be coming to me and saying, 'You've got to get us out of Spain before the fourteenth. If we aren't, United Artists are going to pull out of the film. Speed it up, for God's sake, we're in dire trouble.' I say, 'Yes, Harry, of course.' Then I go on just as I am already. How can I do otherwise?

I'm a fast worker and I can't do better than I am. Then Harry will come to me and say, 'For Christ's sake, I told you we have to be out of here by the fourteenth. What's happened?' I look him straight in the eye and say, 'But Harry, I thought you meant the twenty-fourth, not the fourteenth. If only I'd known you meant the fourteenth I'd have rushed.'"

He lit a cigarette and shrugged. "That's what I mean. You've got to act like an idiot all the time. This, and not the filming, is the frustrating thing. The only compensation is that you are acting like an idiot to Harry Saltzman, and Harry is acting like an idiot to United Artists, and UA is acting like an idiot to the banks . . . all down the line."

He began to talk about his early days as a director, and once more he gave a cynical shrug.

"D'you think you get to be a director because you have talent?" he asked. "Well, admittedly it is one of the qualities you need. But what's more important is pull—or blackmail."

We were interrupted while his assistant came over to discuss the call for the morrow. Hamilton said he was still thinking about it. When he had gone, he took another draft of the raw Rioja and said:

"Did I ever tell you how I blackmailed them into making me a director? I was twenty-eight years old and the best assistant director in the business. I knew that because of the salary Alex Korda and London Films were paying me, and also because Carol Reed always asked for me when we made a film. I'd decided I was going to be a director before I was thirty and Korda kept promising he would give me a chance, but would always add: 'But not until after this film, dear boy. Finish this one, and then we'll see.' He was smart. He knew that good assistants are much harder to find than directors. Then while we were doing *The Third Man* in Vienna, Carol Reed told me it really was about time I struck out on my own. 'I've taught you all you'll ever learn,' he said. 'Go off and make your own mistakes.' I went to Korda and he gave me the same old syrup. 'Just finish this one, darling, we'll see.' I was too late to refuse because I'd already signed my contract, but I swore this really would be the last time."

The next Carol Reed film was *Outcast of the Islands* and it was made partly in Ceylon. The fact that Hamilton fell deeply in love with her and later married her cannot have been entirely unconnected with the decision he took about his career.

"It so happened that my contract with Korda always came up around Christmas Eve," Hamilton said. "That Christmas Eve we were right out there in Ceylon, and when the time came to sign I went up to Carol and said: 'This is it. I'm not going to sign with you again.' Carol Reed said: 'My God, but we're right in the middle. You're doing to me what I once did to Basil Dean.' I said: 'I can't help that. The time has come.' Carol said: 'All right, if you're determined, I'll write out the cable you should send to Korda.'"

They went up to Reed's room and he drafted a cable which said: IF YOU WANT ME TO SIGN AGAIN AND STAY ON AS ASSISTANT HERE YOU HAVE GOT TO KEEP YOUR PROMISE. MY NEXT FILM I WILL DIRECT MYSELF.

Several days passed in which Hamilton gnawed his nails and wondered. Then one day, during a scene on the beach, he saw the production manager approaching with a cable in his hand. He gave it to Carol Reed, who read it and then called Hamilton over with the words:

"You'd better read this."

It was a cable to Reed from Korda, and it said:

YOU PUT HIM UP TO IT YOU BASTARD. TELL HIM ALL RIGHT I PROMISE. HE WILL DIRECT HIS OWN FILM AFTER THIS.

I said:

"That's pretty mild blackmail."

Hamilton grinned. "Ah, but the story isn't finished," he said. "Korda had taken the decision, but it had to be ratified by the board of London Films. Now it so happened that the most powerful man on the board was Sir Arthur Jarratt, now dead, and it would be an exaggeration to say that he was one of my greatest admirers. During World War II Jarratt was in the navy too, as I was, but he saw somewhat less of the salt water than I did—and I expect I sometimes made some remarks about it. Anyway."

He paused. We looked out of the tent. There may have been no salt in it, but the landscape was a sea of mud.

"Anyway. When Korda passed the recommendation to the board, Arthur Jarratt rose in fury to his full four foot six and said: 'Not on your life. That man is not going to direct any film for us. He hasn't the experience. I don't trust his competence. Nothing doing.' So back came a letter from Korda saying how sorry he was, but what could he do, and I had better start thinking of being an assistant again. A melancholy moment, I can tell you."

He shook his head at the memory of it, and then suddenly grinned. "But then I got to thinking. During the filming in Vienna of *The Third Man* Carol Reed had been asked by the directors of London Films for his ideas about the musical accompaniment to the film, and he had replied at once with a marvelous inspiration which had come to him. A few days later he got a telegram from Jarratt: YOUR IDEA ALL RIGHT FOR CABARET SCENE BUT KEEP THAT BANJO OUT OF REST OF FILM. That was how the zither music almost *didn't* become the theme music and the great talking point of The Third Man."

The assistant interrupted us again to point out that time was getting on and a decision had to be made about tomorrow's call. Hamilton looked out at the weather.

"Let's wrap it up for the time being," he said, "and go back to civilization. Give the boys the day off tomorrow and let's start night shooting in San Sebastián in the evening."

The assistant hurried out to spread the good news. Guy Hamilton turned back to me.

"Where was I? Yes, well Carol got this stupid telegram from Jarratt and he flung it down on the ground in disgust. Of course he was determined not to take any notice of it. I reached down and picked it up—I don't know why. I must have a witch in my ancestry. I kept it too. And when I got the news from Korda that Jarratt was blocking my directorship, I went into my files and I dug it out. Not only that. I managed to get the news to Jarratt that if he continued to block me, some newspaper somewhere was going to have solid evidence to prove what a clot he had been over the music for The Third Man. So then I got a telegram. CONGRATULATIONS, it said, YOU ARE OUR NEWEST DIRECTOR. REGARDS. ARTHUR."

He grinned. "So that's how I got to be a director—through sheer talent—for blackmail."

Harry Saltzman had arrived when we got back to San Sebastián and that night we went to dinner at a restaurant reputed to be the best in the city.

"Let's talk about anything but films or the weather," Saltzman said. "I've had a sickener of them today."

On the way in from the airfield at Biarritz his car had skidded on the wet road into a tree and smashed up the driver and a Spanish member of the unit. Later, speaking to the *Play Dirty* unit at Almería, he had been told that they had begun plowing up the desert because so much grass and flowers had sprouted as a result of the rain. The film was so much behind schedule that its star, Michael Caine, would not be able to make his date in *The Battle of Britain* and a new role would have to be adapted for him.

All three wives were now in San Sebastián, Jackie Saltzman, Kerima Hamilton and Ginette Fisz, a willowy, charming and amusing French girl who spoke with a delightful accent and liked to tell everyone that "eet was necessary for me to break my leg before Benny would make me—how you say?—an honest woman." (He had in fact proposed to her while she lay on a stretcher after a skiing accident in Norway.) Ginette Fisz is a golden-haired blonde and she provided just the right contrast to the two striking brunettes.

We had Tad Szulc of the *New York Times* with us and since he was on reassignment from Madrid to Poland, we talked for a time about Eastern Europe.

"At least I'm going to Warsaw if they'll only give me a visa," Szulc said. "Trouble is, I was born in Poland and I speak the language, and they don't go for that too much. They've been stalling for months. If it doesn't work out I'll have to go to Czechoslovakia and I don't want that."

Saltzman said: "Why not? Things are happening there. Big things. Anything might come of it."

"Ah, but Poland's where the real action is going to be. God, I hope I get my visa," Szulc said.*

Jackie Saltzman said: "Harry, don't let's talk politics."

So we went back to talking about films. As usual, Harry Saltzman ate by sight alone, sending each of his dishes back with only the merest taste. And that night, all of us tossed in bed with violent pains and felt considerably shaken next morning.

Saltzman was feeling fine, of course. He called his producer and his director in for a long conference. There were rumors after it was over that Rex Harrison was joining the cast, and that the other stars would include Sir Michael Redgrave, Curt Jurgens, Sir Ralph Richardson, Sir Laurence Olivier and Robert Shaw. But when I asked Hamilton if this were true, he snapped back:

"That's what they keep saying! But there's nothing definite. They can't pin them down. And I can't make my plans until they do." He grimaced angrily. "Why don't they just push those bloody actors into a corner, ask them to say definitely Yes or No, and then make them put their X's on the dotted line?"

Derek Coyte was striding around the hotel saying:

"Who's going to be the girl in the film? Who's the female star? That's what I want to know. I've *got* to have a girl's name in the list when I make the announcement."

---

* Fortunately for him, he didn't. He was posted to Prague instead, just in time for the Russian invasion of Czechoslovakia.

Someone said: "How about Millicent Messerschmitt? Or Harriet Hurricane?"

"I like the big girls," said someone else. "Why not Hy Heinkel, the Brunette Bomb Burst?"

That night and the following night San Sebastián changed into a quarter of Berlin in 1940. Swastikas and German notices hung from the buildings. An entrance to Ruhleben U-Bahn (subway station) had been built into the sidewalk. Prewar German cars drove along the streets, directed by German polizei, and hordes of Spanish extras in the uniforms and female fashions of the day strolled under the lights. It looked more genuinely like Berlin than any part of Berlin does today.

The Spanish authorities cooperated magnificently. The scene included an air raid and a mad rush of the crowd for the shelters. This was a large section of a populated city, but the Spaniards allowed air-raid sirens to be sounded—not once but several times through the night—and doused the lights for the blackout that followed.

Yet that morning the Spanish papers were filled with more attacks on Britain over the Gibraltar question. It was hard to believe that the campaign was directed by the same government whose bomber force was flying free for *The Battle of Britain* and whose cities, railway stations and ports were being taken over by the film company.

As It Was in 1940

———————◆———————

Another week of continuous raids on Keith Park's airfields would almost certainly have turned the scales in Germany's favor in the last days of August 1940. True, scores of German bombers were being shot down every day: not as many as the daily reports claimed, but enough to force Göring to limit his officers to one per bomber crew, in order to save pilots.

But the RAF was in a bad way, too, with less reserves to fall back on than the Germans.

Dowding was afterward to say that each night from August 20 onward, he was praying for a miracle.

On the night of August 24, he got one. The Luftwaffe bombed London.

VIII

Furor Teutonicus

JUST BEFORE THE company finished its Spanish sequences I went back to France, and by the time I caught up with *The Battle of Britain* again in England several crises were threatening to blow up in the producers' faces. Most important was the crisis over money, for the film was not even a quarter way through and only $1,000,000 remained of the original $8,000,000 budget. Would United Artists advance any more? Then there was the buildup of tension among technicians and pilots of the flying unit, now operating out of Duxford and Debden, and the rumbling threat of a walkout. There was the little matter of how to cope with the husband of Princess Margaret as well as the man who nearly married her, both of whom were about to visit the company. There were stirrings in Whitehall and the Establishment over some of the harsher criticisms of the brass hats in the film, and pressures were beginning to be exerted.

For the moment all these were time bombs which would not explode immediately, but one which

looked like going off at any moment concerned Adolf
Galland and the incident of the Nazi salute in the
Göring Train Sequence.

Galland's anger over Hamilton's treatment of this
scene had heated up rather than cooled down after
his departure from San Sebastián. At the beginning of
April, just before he left for a trip to Canada, the general telephoned Colonel Brustellin, his technical expert, to find out whether the offering salute had actually got into the scene. When Brustellin admitted
that it had, Galland said:

"Tell Guy Hamilton it has got to come out. I demand it."

Hamilton's extremely impolite rejoinder to this was
diluted by the gentle Brustellin when he conveyed it
to Galland, but it was still a refusal. So on April 17,
1968, the general wrote a letter to Ben Fisz:

Dear Ben,
    Guy Hamilton has asked Brustellin to let me know that
he is not willing to accept my "technical advice" on the
Göring-Kesselring-Osterkamp scene at the special train
and to have Kesselring render the military and *not* the
"Nazi" or *"deutschen Gruss."*
    The historical facts are absolutely clear and need not
even be discussed. Besides, Guy Hamilton expressed his
dislike of my strong objection on March 30, 1968, shooting location.
    I thought I had enough reason to make clear to you the
same evening my considerations and doubts about a possible distortion of the German side through an exaggerated
display of "furor nazisticus" and about an exaggeration of
the type and cut of military uniforms and of Nazi party
formations and uniforms including the SS, influenced by
the political caricature of the last thirty years, on inap-
propriate occasions.
    Guy Hamilton's decision which was passed on to me

proves that there is good reason for my serious concerns.

If, therefore, the company and the producers are of the opinion that they cannot accept my "technical advice" in the case mentioned above, I am asking to be released from my contract of February 4, 1967, with all the consequences in accordance with para 10, page 5. I wish to point out in particular that, according to para 12(b), page 7, my name must then not be used in any kind of relation with the film nor may my activity as consultant be mentioned.

I may, therefore, ask you to please let me have your decision as soon as possible.

I should regret it if I were forced to this step in the interests of the fairness of such a great film and of a historically so important period of time which I have to guarantee with my name and my image to a large extent not only in Germany.

Besides, I should feel sorry if I could no longer fight with you and if I should have to lose your friendship and that of many others busy on this film so soon.

Sincerely,
Adolf Galland

Wing Commander Stanford-Tuck telephoned Ben Fisz and stressed the seriousness of the situation.

"He means it, you know," he said. "He's good and mad. And don't forget, if he does resign he'll call a press conference to say why."

That was what the producers feared, and they made no secret of their concern. Interest in *The Battle of Britain* had been stimulated in Germany by dozens of articles and news stories emphasizing that this was one war film where the Germans would not be traduced nor caricatured. As a result, German movie theaters were lining up to book the film, and United Artists predicted a success for it which would outstrip that of the Bond films.

On the other hand, Harry Saltzman was only too

aware of how a potential success might be turned into a certain flop by the wrong sort of handling.

"Which was the only country in the world where *The Sound of Music* flopped?" he asked. "Germany. Why? Because the Germans in it were turned into figures of farce."

How could Galland's ultimatum be dealt with—without removing the offending salute from the film? For that Guy Hamilton was determined to retain, and the producers knew they would have an even more disastrous resignation on their hands if they insisted on cutting it. In any case, both Fisz and Saltzman realized the effectiveness of the scene with the Nazi salute included, and were confident that it was correct in spirit if not in fact. But the possible consequences of their stand were not pleasant to contemplate, especially with United Artists breathing nervously down their necks.

Nonetheless, no action was taken about Galland's letter—despite further hints of trouble via Stanford-Tuck—until early in May, when the German newsmagazine *Der Spiegel* printed an article about *The Battle of Britain* and included an interview with Galland. Most of the objections to the original script were set out without any indication whatever that nearly all of them had been met and the script corrected where it had been genuinely at fault. The article ended with the words:

"Last week Galland decided he couldn't take it any longer. During the filming of a Göring scene, Galland sprang in front of the camera and stopped the film. The technical director will make no more compromises. Unless the scene is taken out, he is getting out himself."

On the day the magazine arrived in London, Harry Saltzman called a conference to discuss the situation in his office in Audley Square, in London's Mayfair, and I went along to listen. Besides Fisz there were three other people present: Derek Coyte, the publicity director, Derek Wood, the coauthor of a book on the Battle of Britain called *The Narrow Margin*, and a representative of United Artists in Germany who had flown in that morning.

Saltzman's office is a nutbrown-paneled room with leather sofa and armchairs, a few shelves crammed with books and scripts, a café au lait carpet, no pictures on the walls, small tables with telephones on them, and a desk also covered with telephones. I counted six altogether, and they rang at regular intervals for the next sixty minutes with calls from all over the world. At one time there was an additional interruption from two TV men, a French cameraman and his sound assistant, who were doing a profile of Saltzman for French television. For a large part of the conversation they pointed their camera at the see-through space in the middle of Saltzman's desk; when he sat down, he immediately slipped off his shoes and played footie-footie with his own stockinged feed as we talked.

"We've read the article in *Der Spiegel*," said Saltzman, "and we know what Galland is complaining about. The question is, has Galland got a point? Is his complaint correct? Did Kesselring give the Nazi salute?"

Fisz: "We have photos."

Saltzman: "Not of this incident, you haven't. I've seen pictures of German airmen giving the Nazi salute in Paris. But that was later. Did anyone in the Luftwaffe do it in 1940?"

Coyte: "But is that the point? Guy's trying to be symbolic. He's singling out Kesselring as a Nazi under the skin."

Fisz: "May I say something? You know Galland

144

was given the script and he wrote down comments on every page and every word. But he didn't mention this."

Saltzman (drily): "It wasn't exactly spelled out clearly at that point, was it?" He turned to the German representative of United Artists. "Are you worried about this, Helmut?"

Helmut: "Naturally I don't want trouble, especially with Galland and people like that." He looked depressed, and then shook himself. "But if you are sincere in this scene, I do not know what we have to fear. Besides, we have already signed contracts."

Saltzman: "That won't help us if the people turn against us. Our strong point on this film is that we are being absolutely straightforward and honest—showing how it was—with both the Germans and the British. It is our strong point. But we have to be sure of our ground."

The telephone rang and Saltzman started talking to someone in Paris. While he was doing so, the conversation went on.

Coyte: "If Galland calls a press conference to say he's walked out, it will cause headlines all over Germany."

Wood: "Headlines here too. It's a good story. Can you imagine what the *Daily Express* could do with it?"

Helmut: "If Galland calls a conference and starts being unpleasant, then I think we have to call a conference too."

Saltzman had put down the telephone.

"Let's try to avoid that if we can," he said.

Helmut: "It would be a simple thing for me to call up Augstein [editor-in-chief of *Der Spiegel*] and ask him to send someone to interview Guy Hamilton and see some of the film."

Saltzman: "Oh, gee, no! Anything might happen. You don't know Guy."

Coyte: "From the German point of view, if Galland calls a conference—and he is a German, after all—shouldn't we have a German to reply to him and explain what we're trying to do? It's going to be a lot better than an Englishman doing it. But who is the German we can get to do it? Under the circumstances, other than the fact that Kesselring was a party member we have nothing factual in this case."

Saltzman: "Yes, there must be someone who can stand up to Galland in Germany—but who is he?"

Fisz: "Milch? He was his senior officer."

Helmut (shocked): "But Milch was a Nazi. A convicted war criminal. I don't see how . . ."

Fisz: "What else can we do?"

Saltzman: "We can show Galland the scene on film. I'm not prepared to send it over to Germany, but if he likes to come here—maybe he'll change his mind when he sees it."

Fisz: "But if he sees it, he threatens to bring his lawyer along."

Saltzman: "He can bring his grandmother along for all I care. But let's show it to him."

The telephone rang again and he picked it up.

Some days later Adolf Galland arrived at Pinewood Studios. He had brought a young man along with him, too young to have been in World War II, whom he introduced as his lawyer. In preparation for trouble, Fisz had called in reinforcements and this time, in addition to Derek Wood and Derek Coyte, also present were Group Captain Tom Gleave, an ex-Battle of Britain pilot and now an air force department historian, and Air Commodore James Wallace, ex-wartime pilot, one-time deputy captain of the queen's flight. The array of talent at once put Galland on the defensive, and when defensive he becomes belligerent.

But any tendency to flare on this occasion was kept suavely under control by his lawyer, anxious to make it clear that they wanted to be friendly and cooperative. He listened to Galland venting some old-time grievances about RAF fliers (whom he had helped when they had been shot down in France, and who had shown him scant gratitude in their memoirs) and efficiently guided him on to other subjects.

Finally, after several coffees, we walked across the studio to the theater where they were waiting to show us the sequence.

Once it had begun, one wondered how it could have been visualized any other way. Coming as it did as the culminating point of Göring's disastrous visit, the last scene with its Nazi salute seemed not only logical but inevitable. It soon became evident that Galland's legal adviser was on our side; he had obviously not realized that the German sequences would be genuinely German, with German actors speaking their own language. Almost immediately the sequence was finished, Ben Fisz ordered it to be shown again, and while we waited the lawyer whispered to Galland:

"I think anyone who objected to this could become the laughingstock of Germany."

At the end of the second run-through, we realized that Galland's mood had completely changed. He was impressed, there was no doubt of it. He would not have been human had he not been pleased to see that Falke (who was a thinly disguised version of himself) had been given one of the best moments in the sequence; and he was intelligent enough to realize that Guy Hamilton, no matter what his feeling about Germany, had directed the whole with scrupulous care and authenticity. Since he could not give in without one small protest, he said:

"I still think the Kesselring salute isn't necessary."

The lawyer interposed hurriedly: "We couldn't possibly, however, advise you to do anything about it."

We adjourned to a long and amiable lunch, after which Galland and his lawyer were seen to the car which was to take them to the airport and the afternoon plane back to Germany.

The general shook everyone by the hand and grinned amiably.

"Let us forget all the quarrels of the past," he said. "Let us start from scratch as if nothing has happened."

He climbed into the car and leaned his head through the window.

"Until the next time," he said.

We waited until he had gone, and then Fisz said:

"I wonder what he means by 'the next time'? The next meeting—or the next quarrel?"

As It Was in 1940

In the new phase of bombing which the Luftwaffe was unleashing against the RAF and its installations in August 1940, Reichsmarschall Göring had told his pilots that everything was open to them, with one exception. They could and should hit factories, oil depots, air bases, railway centers and vital road junctions.

"There will no longer be any restrictions upon the choice of targets," he told them.

There was, however, one embargo. London. He told his Luftwaffe chiefs that under no circumstances must the British capital be bombed nor should any overt attack be made upon purely civilian targets. Hitler had given the order personally. He was well aware of the impact upon the neutral world—especially the United States—which a bombing of London would have. There was one story in circulation already that Winston Churchill walked out into the blackout every night in London and raised his arms to the sky, crying: "Why don't you come? Bomb us, bomb us!"

Churchill was convinced that only by reading of London bombed, its monuments destroyed, its citizens killed, would the Americans understand what the war was all about and come in on Britain's side.

Göring was far too wily to fall into the trap and ordered his bombers to keep away.

But on August 24, during an all-out attempt to hit every vital installation in southeast England, the Luftwaffe made a mistake. It was after darkness had fallen. A day of raids all over Kent and the Thames estuary was followed by attacks from some 170 German bombers, among which was a formation which had been ordered to drop bombs on the port of Rochester, on the Thames, and the great cluster of oil stores at Thameshaven.

Two of the bombers, harried by RAF nightfighters and rocked by a barrage of antiaircraft fire, strayed off course. They were in such fear of being hit that their pilots decided that the best course was to jettison their bombs and get out fast. They did so.

The bombs fell on central and inner London. Houses were smashed and fires burned at Islington, Millwall, Stepney, Tottenham, Finsbury, East Ham and Bethnal Green. About a hundred men, women and children were killed.

LONDON BOMBED, announced American reporters, and the British censor—who usually cracked down on the location of bomb hits—made no attempt to stop the news from going out. NAZI BOMBS KILL BRITISH KIDS, said a New York headline.

Göring was furious. "Major Josef Knobel remembers very clearly the telegram from Göring which arrived early next morning," recalled one German flier, Cajus Bekker. "It was sent to all the bomber units which had been in action the previous night. 'An immediate report is required identifying those crews who dropped bombs within the perimeter of London. Luftwaffe High Command will itself undertake the *punishment of each aircraft captain involved. They will be posted to infantry regiments.'"*

As for Winston Churchill, it would be wrong to say that he was pleased. His beloved London had been hit. Men, women and children had died. But he was certainly not cast down by the catastrophe.

On the contrary, he sat down immediately to work out how best to exploit it for the benefit of his beleaguered Britain.

IX

Enter Townsend
and Snowdon

————————◆————————

GROUP CAPTAIN PETER Townsend arrived for his first
visit to *The Battle of Britain* during the shooting in
San Sebastián. He was in the throes of writing his
own account of the battle (during which he flew both
Hurricanes and Spitfires) and would do a lecture tour
in the U.S. in 1969 to publicize the film. Save for a
few flecks of gray in his wavy black hair he had
hardly changed from the young man whose photograph was always in the newspapers in the 1950s. It
was hard to believe that he was fifty-four years old
and the father of five.

He was quite the politest man I have ever met,
even when the Spanish reporters started to ask him
questions about his relationship with Princess Margaret.

"You really must not ask me anything about that,
mon vieux," he would say, smiling gently. "You
wouldn't want me to embarrass other people, would
you, any more than you would want to embarrass
me."

But about anything else he talked endlessly, about his childhood, his air battles, his travels, in a soft monotone which did not change even when he was describing the shooting down of his first Heinkel. He posed for pictures with Galland, with Hein Riess in his Göring uniform, and with the Messerschmitts, and showed no sign of impatience while the cameras were clicking. He was always first to a door to hold it open for anyone, male or female, who was passing through. He handed money out to street urchins and smiled and listened with every sign of attentiveness when middle-aged women, complete strangers, came across the room and gushed over him. One began to understand why he had won so many hearts during his service with the royal family.

He brought his Belgian wife, Marie Luce, with him to Spain and though she mostly wore a raincoat and headscarf against the rigors of a Basque spring, she was an elegant and good-looking woman, and vastly different in appearance from Princess Margaret—tall, leggy and almost as self-effacing as her husband. Cool was the adjective I was tempted to apply to her until I remembered Peter Townsend's story of how she broke down and panicked just before their marriage.

Just after they had decided to get married they had gone to stay at a house on Cap Benat, in the south of France, taking Marie Luce's mother along as a chaperone. Someone in Belgium leaked the news and also where they were staying, and hordes of reporters and cameramen rushed down to the Var to get pictures and stories of the couple. Townsend was not entirely surprised, for he had undergone a similar siege in Sussex in 1952 at a time when it was rumored that he was about to elope with Princess Margaret; but he still chides himself for his failure to realize what a shock it would be to his bride-to-be. "She had never for a moment realized that this would be of interest to anyone but our immediate families," he said. "She could not believe that, for the most ridiculous of reasons, we were public figures."

It is typical of Townsend that instead of calling for the police he eventually decided to invite the newspapermen into the house and told them he would answer any "reasonable" questions. The moment they surged on to the terrace of the house, Marie Luce panicked. She heard the cameramen asking for her and dashed into the house, and when one or two of them came after her, she decided that only flight would save her.

"Silly girl," said Townsend. "They were quite decent fellows really, and only doing their job. But all the while they were talking to me, I could see Marie Luce madly scrambling down the cliffs toward the sea. Then shortly afterwards, I saw to my horror that she had got into a small dinghy and was rowing away out to sea. It wasn't the calmest of days, in more ways than one, and I was terrified because I knew Marie Luce was no good whatsoever at rowing. I kept telling myself that I had got to get away and go down to her rescue, and all the time I had to go on being polite to the newspapermen. It seemed hours before I could get them off my hands, and then I rushed down the cliff, got a motorboat and went off to rescue Marie Luce."

He added: "Thank goodness she doesn't have to worry about that sort of thing anymore."

He was, alas, being a little too optimistic, but then he didn't know at that time that the man who eventually did marry Princess Margaret, the earl of Snowdon, would also soon be appearing on the sets of *The Battle of Britain*, inevitably reviving speculation about Townsend. A week or two later it so happened that while Townsend was visiting the film once more his wife went for a holiday to the south of France, and one evening I saw her. I was in a car driving through the main square of St. Tropez. She was staring into the door of a news dealer's store, and right at eye level with her was a copy of a French scandal sheet called *France Dimanche*. PETER ET TONY was the flaring headline over a story of how the unsuccessful and the successful suitor for Princess Margaret's hand were working on the same film, and how the producers were desperately trying to keep them from meeting.

They never did meet, of course. Townsend was far too discreet. Nor did he ever mention Snowdon's name or reveal that he was even aware of his existence. As I said before, he was the politest man I have ever met, and in many ways the most decent. All the old clichés like "true blue" and "stiff upper lip," "clean-minded Englishman" and "man of honor" seemed meaningful again as one got to know him.

Anthony Armstrong-Jones, first earl of Snowdon, would obviously have had no objection at all to meeting Townsend and made no secret of his curiosity about the man who had once meant so much to his wife.

"What's he like? What sort of a chap is he?" he would ask when it was mentioned that Townsend had been on the set a day or two previously.

"Not as bright as you, sir," someone said on one occasion.

"Ah, but much nicer, I hear," Snowden said.

He roared with laughter when someone told him the story of Townsend's visit to Field Marshal Milch in Germany, where he had gone seeking information for his book from the old Luftwaffe commander. He had mentioned in the course of conversation that he was intensely fond of mountaineering.

"I'll wager there's one mountain he keeps away from," Milch said, while Townsend was out of the room. "Snowdon."

Snowdon's association with *The Battle of Britain* was an indirect one. He had been commissioned to take a series of photographs of the London blitz sequences in the film, to be published in *Look* magazine.

The blitz was to be a big set piece, a highlight of the film in every sense of the word, and the art department had been told to spare no expense to make it look genuine. They had accordingly bought an old tea warehouse down in dockland which they proposed to destroy with fire and explosives; and for the most important scene in the sequence, where Andy, a sergeant-pilot (played by Ian McShane), comes home just in time to be caught in a raid during which his wife is killed, the Greater London Council had turned over a large tract of Bermondsey to them. It was an area of derelict streets and decaying houses which was scheduled to be demolished under a GLC slum-clearance scheme, and officialdom had no objections to the film company doing part of their work for them. So two experts on death and destruction, Glen Robinson and Cliff Richardson, had been turned loose on rows of mean houses in Dragon Road where they were enthusiastically planting smoke pots, gas tanks (for starting fires) and plastic explosives. It was only a few hours before the main unit was due to move in that they discovered that two of the crumbling houses were still occupied; moreover, the two families who lived there had for months been defying GLC attempts to get them out, and they made it clear in choice Cockney language that a flipping film company was certainly not going to succeed where bureaucracy had failed. They were staying put, blitz or not. So their houses had had to be specially sandbagged, and the production manager, John Palmer, was called out to soothe the aggrieved householders and compensate them for the fire, smoke and noise to come.

When I got to Dragon Road at about 10:00 p.m. on the night of May 9, Snowdon had already arrived and was chatting with a bunch of press photographers from the London papers, and when I came up to them I realized that they were talking about film speeds and exposure problems. I had heard that some of the photographers resented Snowdon thinking his rank and connections got him special facilities, but you would never have guessed it from their attitude now. Everyone was friendly.

I was surprised at Snowdon's small stature. He had the neat, trim figure of a ballet dancer, and he dressed rather like a character in a hunt scene from *Der Freischütz:* very tight trousers, three-quarter jump shoes, a dark patterned shirt topped by a very short-waisted leather jacket. All he needed was a hat with a feather in it. He had an amiable monkey face which more often than not was creased into a most attractive smile, and I was soon to discover that he had a monkey's facility for climbing to the most inaccessible spots in search for an angle: he would scramble over rooftops, shin up scaffolding, lean over

157

from heights with sure-footed ease. For the moment, however, while the setup was being completed, he was waiting, and while waiting he munched on a sausage roll from the unit canteen wagon. Later on we were to find that whenever he was not taking pictures, Snowdon would be eating. "They must never give him any meals at Kensington Palace," someone said, as he crammed down the third sausage roll. He proved to have an insatiable appetite for buns, bacon and hard-boiled eggs, but neither the starch nor the carbohydrates seemed to have any effect upon his lean, obviously superfit body.

Great crowds had descended upon the district to watch the night's shooting but they were kept away from Dragon Road by a rope barrier and a police patrol. On the corner of Dragon Road and George Street was a pub appropriately called the George and Dragon, and local residents as well as members of the unit were allowed through to it; and round about 11.15 p.m. a number of us, including Snowdon, found our way there. Inside the public bar a high old time was being had by all. The locals were knocking back pints of wallop and reminiscing to the reporters about their memories of the blitz (for this part of London, from the Elephant and Castle westward, had been heavily hit by German bombs in 1940). An old character was playing "Knees Up Mother Brown" and "The Lambeth Walk" and other Cockney airs on an out-of-tune piano, and many a beery voice was raised in song. Behind the bar the pubkeeper's young wife, with a Junoesque figure, had dressed in a low-cut black silk dress for the occasion, and Snowdon joined in the raucous cries of appreciation each time she leaned over to pull a glass of ale.

It was during one of these spirited moments that the police walked in.

Closing time for pubs in the Bermondsey area of London is 11:00 p.m. and it was now 11:30. Two burly police constables pushed and shoved their way to the bar, crying "Make way, there!" in their most authoritative voices. The pianist hesitated and suddenly stopped. In the comparative silence which followed, I heard the first constable say, as he leaned over the bar:

"Are you trying to lose your license, madam? Don't you know it's well past closing time?"

Our hostess suddenly looked both surprised and scared. Her husband behind her had gone white. This was their first pub and the brewery to whom they were contracted would never forgive them if they got into trouble.

We had all stopped drinking now, except Snowdon, who seemed completely unaware of what was happening. He had his glass of whisky in his hand and he was sipping it. I noticed that all the reporters were watching him. And then the second policeman turned, saw him, and said:

"Hey, you! Don't you know it's past closing time? Finish up that drink—quick now, no nonsense!"

"Oh God," said Snowdon. "This would have to happen." And then to Derek Coyte, who was standing beside me: "Get me out of here!"

Coyte moved up and bustled the royal photographer through the bar and into the kitchen behind. Meanwhile, the reporters, who had been watching it all, now turned to the police.

"You realize who that was, don't you, officer?" said one of them, eagerly. "What does it feel like to order a member of the royal family out of a bar?"

159

The constables looked at each other, their manner suddenly uncertain.

"'Ere, what is all this?" the first one said, turning back to the pubkeeper's wife.

She explained hurriedly that she had been to see the inspector, that the inspector had given her permission to keep open while the film company was shooting, and . . .

"But who was that?" he asked, indicating the spot where Snowden had been.

"Who was that you chucked out, you mean?" She was regaining her confidence. "Only the earl of Snowdon, that's all."

There was a heavy silence, and the constable said:

"You didn't have no right to keep open down here. If it's a private party, you should be upstairs." He swung round. "All of you. Go on, get upstairs at once and let's have this place closed down."

But the reporters were making for the telephone and in my mind's eye I could already see the headlines in the morning papers:

LORD SNOWDON CAUGHT IN BERMONDSEY PUB RAID.

One thing was certain. Peter Townsend would *never* have found himself in a similar predicament.

Just after midnight Snowdon was persuaded to come out of hiding and join the film party upstairs. He seemed reassured when he was told that Spitfire Films had sent a message to the Press Association explaining that the incident did not concern him, since he was an invited guest of the film company. A fat lot of good that did, of course, but Snowdon cheered up after he had heard it.

"Poor chap," someone said. "Philip's always narking at him for hanging around East End pubs."

"At least he drinks his drinks out of an ordinary glass," said someone else. "Every time I see Philip, he's got his head buried in a bloody great silver cup of champagne."

Together with Harry Saltzman, Ben Fisz and their wives, we moved back to Dragon Road to find Guy Hamilton all but ready to take the scene. There was an old prewar taxi drawn up, ready to run into camera and drop Ian McShane, arriving to seek out his wife. Extras in any old clothes, or nightdresses and pajamas, stood around in groups, clutching bulging suitcases or children with dirt-streaked faces. These were to portray the bombed-out Londoners on their way to the shelters or refuge homes. A large fire engine, genuine but pre-1940, was ticking over with a crew of firemen-extras clutching at hosepipes.

Suddenly the brutes (the great arc lights) were turned on and the whole of Dragon Road was as light as day. And there in the foreground, determined to get into the picture, was Mr. Spring, one of the sitting tenants, a cigarette between his lips. Elaine Schreyeck, the script girl, whispered rapidly to Derek Cracknell, the assistant, who lifted his bullhorn.

"Will that gentleman in the foreground please bury that cigarette?" he said, politely. "They didn't have smokes with spats on in 1940." Mr. Spring hurriedly dropped his cigarette. "Thank you, sir. And now, if you want to appear in this picture, will you please rub some dirt in your face, for Gawd's sake. You look as if you're just back from the barber's."

Mr. Spring looked at the ground, which was very wet and dirty, and then turned on his heel, saying exactly what he thought about *The Battle of Britain* as he walked away.

"All right, guvnor?" Cracknell glanced at Guy Hamilton, who gave him a thumb sign. At the same moment Snowdon scurried across the ground and shinned up a scaffolding post until he was balancing precariously, high above us, beside an arc light. "Okay—turn over—action!" At the other end of the street, a great sheet of flame belched out of the doors and windows of a house. A shattering explosion brought nearby walls smashing down in a whirl of dust. More explosions. Batteries of searchlights came alight and fingered the sky and now we could see that barrage balloons were floating all around us. The sound for this shot would obviously be dubbed in afterward, and so the scene was accompanied by an increasingly frenetic commentary from Cracknell through the bullhorn:

"Okay, bring the ambulance up! Look through the window, Ian! You're amazed at the sight of it—and frightened too! Climb out now, and start threading your way through the evacuees. Come on, evacuees—look lively. Drag the kids! And you kids, start crying and shouting. Come on, ma, don't laugh, this isn't a laughing matter, they're about to blow you to bloody pieces. Cuff that little bleeder with you over the ear and drag him! Come on, now. Go! Go go go go!"

For four or five minutes through the noise of mounting explosions, the increasingly baleful glare, and the mixture of dust and spraying water from the fire engines, the cameras concentrated on the scene. Then Hamilton signaled for a cut, the fires were cut off, the brutes were doused, and Harry Saltzman passed a bottle of whisky around in the darkness. Snowdon came down for a drink and a bacon sandwich.

It went on like that until 4:30 a.m. A flare of flames and a holocaust of bangs, and then a long wait while the charges were reset. This part of London had not had such a gaudy night since the blitz itself. But at 4:30, just when the last shot was set up and the unit was ready to go, the lights were suddenly cut.

"Gee, I'm in trouble here," shouted Cracknell. "We've got a fuse or something."

What they had got, in fact, was a pulled switch. The electricians had promised to work until 4:30 and no one had thought of coming to an arrangement with them when the deadline came. By the time the whole thing was arranged, dawn was coming up fast and it was too late to get a matching shot. Order was given to strike the set, and we all went home.

When last seen, the earl of Snowdon was climbing into his car with yet another sausage roll in his hand, and streaking down the rain-washed streets of Bermondsey toward Kensington Palace and breakfast.

A hearty one, I have no doubt.

As It Was in 1940

———◆———

Herman Göring had always boasted that no British bomber would ever get through his defenses and drop bombs on Berlin. He was so confident that the German capital was safe that he made a boast, which, to the anti-Jewish elements in the Nazi party, had an impact.

"If any British plane ever drops bombs on Berlin," he cried, "you can call me Meyer!"

Winston Churchill remembered this. While his Air Raid Precaution workers were still clearing away the debris created by the accidental German bombing of London on August 24, 1940, he summoned the chiefs of the Royal Air Force. He told them that a reprisal raid must be organized at once.

"The RAF will bomb Berlin," he ordered.

The RAF brass hats tried their best to dissuade him. They hadn't got the planes capable of doing a real job, they said. It was a waste of effort, anyway. What good could it do, bombing a capital city like Berlin, when vital bombs were needed to destroy German military targets?

But Churchill insisted. He knew that a raid by the RAF would humiliate Göring, disgrace the Luftwaffe and infuriate Hitler.

And from that, anything might happen.

164

X

Crisis in the
Air

ROBERT SHAW AND Christopher Plummer joined the cast toward the end of May, and Guy Hamilton looked visibly cheered by their arrival. Though Shaw came with a reputation for being forcefully outspoken over ideas he didn't like and Plummer was known to have sudden fits of temperament, there was absolutely no sign of antistar bias in his attitude toward them. Perhaps it was because he recognized these two self-confident characters as real professionals, and for professionals he had a very healthy respect.

"They can make trouble, just as much as bad actors can," he said. "A shrewd professional can upset the balance of the film even though he is performing brilliantly. That's when you realize that a test of strength is coming. You have to prepare yourself, and the great temptation is to slap him down. But you can only do that when he is wrong. The fatal thing is to slap him down when he is right. A good professional knows himself so well that if you argue, and he is right, you are sunk. So you wait—wait for him to make the slightest mistake—and then you slap him down so hard he doesn't know what hit him. And you're in!"

Watching these two burly characters standing shoulder to shoulder and staring Hamilton straight in the eye, I doubted anyone's ability to slap *them* down. But we should see.

Shaw had, in fact, already demonstrated his independence of mind by going to work on his own part in the script. He had been told that his character was roughly based on that of the late "Sailor" Malan, one of the most successful pilots with the RAF during the Battle of Britain. But the role, as originally conceived, was that of a kind of father figure, a sort of flying Mr. Chips, who treated the members of the squadron he commanded during the battle with paternalistic concern. Shaw at once sent for the files and the reminiscences and soon confirmed his suspicion that "Sailor" Malan was not that kind of a character at all.

"He was ruthless and he was efficient," he said. "He had a black hatred for the Germans. He ran his own squadron like an efficient business, and he despised anyone who wasn't up to the job. He wasn't running a public school, he was in the business of killing Germans—and he was out to get results."

Shaw had readjusted his part accordingly, and it stiffened up the script at just those points where it might have crumpled into sentimentality.

On the morning of Shaw's arrival at North Weald RAF station, where the unit would be filming for a few days, his white Rolls was stopped by a guard with a walkie-talkie and directed behind a hangar. A few minutes later the sky on all sides was filled with ack-ack bursts, a stick of bombs was exploding across the field, a dispersal hut was going up in flames, an oil tank was blazing and Spitfires were racing over the grass trying to avoid the explosions and get airborne. The death-and-destruction boys were on the job again, simulating a German raid on the station.

That afternoon Shaw did his first scene, which was supposed to take place as the aftermath of the raid. His field has been put temporarily out of action. He has lost three of his Spitfires and several of his men. But one German bomber has crashed near the field and pilot and crew taken prisoner. Skipper (Shaw's name in the film) is driving back from an inspection when he sees the prisoners being led in. He climbs out of the car and he is good and mad.

There was one run-through of the scene and you could feel the whole unit relaxing. They were in the presence of a certificated member of the craft.

"That seems to be just right," said Hamilton. "Let's take it, shall we?"

The car drove up again and Shaw climbed out. The camera was running now.

SKIPPER (shouting)

Corporal!

The CORPORAL halts the party as SKIPPER crosses to them.

SKIPPER

And where do you think you're taking those vultures?

CORPORAL

Officer to the mess, sir. NCOs to the guardroom.

SKIPPER

Like hell you are! They made this mess. Let them clean it up!

CORPORAL

What about the officer, sir?

SKIPPER looks at the GERMAN OFFICER.

SKIPPER

Give him a bloody shovel!

It was an effective scene, and it had, in fact, been in the original script. General Galland had objected to it on the grounds that it was in poor taste, but it had stayed in; and now Shaw gave it a savagery that jolted one with its black hate and anger.

After it was over, we went across and joined Ian McShane and Edward Fox who were lounging on deck chairs in front of an RAF dispersal hut, purring in the unexpected afternoon sun. McShane played a sergeant pilot in Skipper's squadron and Fox a long-haired (for those days) flier from the Oxford University Air Squadron. In the film they bickered about class and background between missions, emphasizing the social differences of the time; for McShane's role, of course, though he flew the same planes in the same squadron as did Fox, was that of a noncom who, for purely snob reasons, lacked "officer qualifications."

"Can you imagine a system that allowed it to happen while we were fighting for our lives?" Shaw asked. "He could win the war for us, but he wasn't allowed in the officers' mess!" He grinned with the unworried expression of a character who had never let such social distinctions worry him. "It just shows how things have changed in the past few years though. The last air film I appeared in was *The Dam Busters* and I came up for an audition as one of the pilots. They took a look at my jib and my brawn and waved me away. 'Not officer material,' they said. I played a sergeant. In this film I'm a squadron leader —we're making progress!"

Attached to the unit for all these fighter squadron scenes was a former RAF fighter pilot, Squadron Leader James (Ginger) Lacey, who is generally considered to be the flier who shot down the most enemy aircraft during the Battle of Britain. He had slid into another deck chair during Shaw's remarks and sat twirling his moustache (ginger, naturally) while he listened. After which he said, mildly:

"Some of us were glad to be sergeant pilots, you know." He indicated Fox, who played a languid type. "It kept us apart from amateur clots like this one. We were serious fliers—the professionals."

"In that case," said Shaw, with just the merest flick of asperity, "why did you finally decide to come up in the world and become an officer?"

"Oh," said Lacey, "didn't you know about me? I'm always around for a bit of ready cash. When someone offered me a commission, I discovered that in order to become an officer I would first have to be discharged from the service. Other ranks get a bounty of twenty pounds when they are discharged, and I needed it. So I took the twenty pounds and then I became an officer. Simple as that."

It was obvious that Shaw didn't know whether Lacey was being serious or not.

Since there was a character named Tin Legs among the fighter pilots in *The Battle of Britain* it was inevitable that Douglas Bader, the legless hero of World War II, should turn up on the set. His encounter with Robert Shaw is one which those who saw it will treasure, for it was a meeting of two different worlds.

On May 26 Air Chief Marshal Lord Dowding was invited to Duxford airfield to see the planes and meet the actors, and a number of old Battle of Britain pilots had agreed to come too: Al Deere, Stanford-Tuck, Ginger Lacey, Brian Kingcombe were all there. In a way, *The Battle of Britain* was Dowding's vindication. He had been shamefully treated by the RAF and the government after the battle was over, and thanks to some shoddy maneuvers had been deprived of the credit he deserved for the victory. He had been shunted off into retirement with scant thanks for his efforts; the loyal commander of one of the two fighter groups which he controlled during the battle, Keith Park, had transferred to a training post; whereas the commander of the other group, Leigh-Mallory, who had repeatedly disobeyed his orders during the battle, got Park's former group.

It was a nasty business altogether, and *The Battle of Britain* had, as one of its aims, the presentation of the facts as they had actually happened. His approaching rehabilitation seemed to have given a new lease of life to Dowding. He was eight-six years old and confined to a wheelchair with arthritis, but he had submitted to two operations for cataracts so that he might see something of the progress of the film. The more he was consulted about the script, the more eager he became to break the silence he had imposed on himself since 1940 about his humiliation.

He had decided at long last to write his autobiography, as the result of which all the skeletons in the RAF cupboard, so long locked away, were likely to come out and be rattled.

Because he had been one of the favorite pilots of Leigh-Mallory, Douglas Bader was not exactly Dowding's model hero, and some wry looks were cast in his direction when he insisted on pushing the old man around in his wheelchair during his inspection of the planes. Dowding remarked tetchily at one point that "the battle might have gone considerably better if junior officers had not exercised undue influence on their seniors at certain critical moments." If this was aimed at him, Bader chose to ignore it. He made it clear to all and sundry that Dowding was his superhero. When he was introduced to Robert Shaw, he pointed at the old man and said:

"If it hadn't been for him, old boy, we might be digging salt out of a Silesian salt mine. Those bloody Kraut airplanes over there with all that language written over them—that's what we would be speaking. At least I wouldn't, I'd probably be dead, but your generation would."

He was obviously a type of hero which Shaw and Plummer, who had joined him, had never really imagined existed in real life. He was out of a book by John Buchan. There was no doubt of his heroic stature. He had fought his way back into the RAF despite the loss of both his legs and by sheer guts overcome the pain and the handicap to make himself one of the most skillful pilots in the battle. He was never crushed by anyone or anything; even while a prisoner of the Germans he had never knuckled under to them nor disguised his antipathy toward them.*

In late middle age, Bader was still a belligerent bulldog of a man determined to show the world that nothing and no one was going to hinder him or silence him. He would respond to any challenge, even when it was unspoken. It was he who pushed Dowding's wheelchair, though he had two wooden legs himself; and between 10:00 a.m. and lunchtime he never sat down once. When the camerman clamored to photograph him against a Hurricane, he immediately said:

"How about one of me in the cockpit? For old time's sake."

A member of the unit at once moved forward to help him, but Al Deere reached out a restraining hand.

---

* This was one of Galland's grievances. He had treated Bader well when he was captured and had received scant thanks for it.

"For God's sake don't do it," he said. "Douglas isn't a man who likes to be helped. He'll punch you in the nose if you touch him."

So we hung back and the legless hero balanced himself against the side of the Hurricane, glowering at it with a Churchillian outjut of his jaw, as if the plane were challenging him. Suddenly he swung his right wooden leg, with a sort of circular flick, so that the boot on the end caught in the stirrup on the side of the plane; he reached forward, pulled with mighty strength and a second later was up and on the wing and then swinging into the cockpit. It was an incredible exhibition of agility, coordination and strength, and the cameramen were delighted. After he had posed, grinning, for a few minutes one of them shouted:

"Now would you do the same in a Messerschmitt, sir?"

Bader said:

"First I've got to work something out. I've got to try and remember how I ever got out of this bloody plane!" He paused, shamming deep thought, hand on chin. "Oh, yes, I remember now!"

The hands gripped each side of the cockpit, the body rose, the legs flipped sideways in a whiplash and then clattered down, and he was standing on the wing. He smiled at the scatter of applause and climbed to the ground.

"Now," he said, "let's go and do the same to the Kraut."

After it was over, he rejoined Robert Shaw and presently an interviewer from the British Broadcasting Corporation came up. The TV cameras turned on them. In the next few minutes, Shaw took no part in the conversation—not vocally, anyway. But the expression on his face was eloquent enough. He had obviously never realized that anyone in real life really talked like this.

Interviewer: "Douglas Bader, here we are, surrounded by German aircraft on an RAF field which must be quite a shock to you. Now there are people who say, after a quarter of a century, why make this film, why bring it all up again? What do you feel about it?"

Bader: "Well it's history, old boy, one must show history. If you can show history in a film it's better than in the history books, and it'll be in those things anyway. By all means let's show it in a film, but all I beg the *Battle of Britain* producers not to do is to make it so that the Germans win the Battle of Britain, because they didn't. They may try to make out that they did now it's all over, but they didn't in fact."

Interviewer: "In a word, Douglas, what's your message as we stand here all this time on your old airfield, surrounded by the Hurricanes which you flew out of here . . .

Badger: "Not Hurricanes, Spitfires which I flew out of here, Ms-109s which I shot down from out of here . . ."

Interviewer: "And all these 109s around here—what message do you hope that the film and these planes and you can give now, this year, about the Battle of Britain? Everything is sweetness and light between Britain and Germany now. Is it right to bring it up, to remind everybody of the old war and the old animosity?"

Bader: "Well, why not? Why not film history? Surely the lesson one learns is that one forgives but that one doesn't forget. It's as simple as that."

Interviewer: "When you were up there in your plane fighting, Douglas, what were you thinking?"

"Bader: "Well, I was thinking about what I was going to do when I got back in the evening. That was what I was thinking, old boy."

Interviewer: "Even when you were up in the air?"

Bader: "Yes."

Interviewer: "Was it us and them, or was it your machine against their machines?"

Bader looked at him for a moment as if he was crazy, and we waited for the epithets about the Krauts to come out. But he restrained himself.

Bader: "No, it was the airplanes one sort of felt badly about. I loathe those crooked swastikas. What was it Churchill said: 'The crooked cross of Nazi infamy.' That's what one hated. Coming into our skies and dropping bombs on our country and so on. It wasn't personal. You can't hate a chap you can't see, although we all hated the idea of Hitler and the things he did. I mean he was identifiable—but the airplanes were just airplanes and when you saw them go up in smoke one was delighted and one never thought about anyone being inside them, you know."

Interviewer: "Were you surprised when you found all these old machines assembled here?"

Bader: "Very surprised to see them here at Duxford, old boy. My old station. They wouldn't have been if the Socialist government hadn't disbanded RAF Fighter Command. Did you see that picture in the newspapers the other day of these 109s flying over the cliffs of Dover on their way here? I remember thinking that if the government hadn't disbanded Fighter Command a fortnight ago, those K . . . those planes wouldn't have flown over the cliffs of Dover— even now. We'd have gone out and we'd have shot the bleeders down."

Interviewer: "Thank you, Douglas Bader."

Bader turned and put his hands to his nose and sniffed them.

"You know, even if I was blind, I'd know I'd been in a bloody Kraut kite. You can tell by their smell!"

He hobbled away, waving a hand.

"I can't wait to see the film," he shouted. "It's going to be good. Historical. Only don't let the Krauts win it. We won the Battle of Britain—not them!"

Robert Shaw looked after him for a long moment and then turned away.

"I never knew people *talked* like that," he said.

While the first unit was shooting ground scenes at Duxford, the air unit moved to Debden airfield, some twenty minutes away, and from there the hard work went on of getting the air battle sequences into the can. It did not get any easier as the days went on, and the weather, once more, was no help. In that dark wet dreadful summer of 1968, no place was darker or wetter than this part of Cambridgeshire. Whenever a forecast gave any hope at all, the planes were warmed up and made ready; there was a briefing each morning, rain or shine, so that the pilots knew what they were supposed to do; and the moment there was a break in the sky, up went the Psychedelic Monster and the two fleets of fighters, to seek the blue reaches of the upper air and begin their complicated maneuvers. Everyone was well aware by this time that fighting air battles during the Battle of Britain was one thing, but getting them on to camera was proving to be something else again. One evening I sat in the makeshift cinema at Duxford to see a selection of scenes taken from the B-25, the twin-seater Messerschmitt and Spitfire, and one of the Heinkels specially rigged for camera work. They looked exciting enough to me, but they lacked a beginning and an end, and they gave no sense of identification. Until they were knitted into the narrative of the film, and until there were shots showing who was flying what, and on what kind of mission, one was left, so to speak, in the air. I presumed that this would be remedied by work in the studio and the interpolation of close-ups of the actor-pilots concerned. But during the session I was aware of a silent protest going on behind me, and when I emerged I fell in with a member of the art department who had been watching the rushes. He was a Polish sketch artist named Maciek Piotrowski, and he had been a fighter pilot both in his own country in 1939 and in Britain during the battle.

He exuded unhappiness in the unspoken but obvious way which only Poles can when they were acutely distressed. I asked him why. He shrugged eloquently and said:

"You saw why. Those rushes. Is that supposed to be the Battle of Britain? Are those planes supposed to be flown by men fighting for their lives, and knowing they have to kill or be killed? Did you see how they attacked?" He made a gesture of his hand, as if a bus were turning a corner. "They came round like this! And during the battle, that was not the case at all. When we turned, we had to do it very quickly. So we just turned on our backs"—he flipped his hand—"so! and did it by the short route. It took only one-hundredth of the time to do it. And what we needed always was time and space—and there was no space once we were fighting over the Channel, the sky was very crowded with your own boys and the enemy. If you had tried to turn like they do, you would have banged into someone. We did the fighter turn, a half-roll and then just pull back the stick. But where is the fighter turn in those rushes? Ah, it hurts me. I want to cry."

We walked in silence for a moment, and then he said:

"I don't blame the pilots. How can they know? They have never been in an air battle—except Santa Cruz, perhaps, and he—well, never mind, he is a good flier, but he hasn't experienced the real battles, either. So until someone tells them and makes them do it, they will continue to fly not like fighters but like—*bombers!*" The way he said the word made it sound a shameful thing. "Slow, contrived, lumbering. And when you see those contrived shots on the screen, everything is like yesterday's warmed-up schnitzel. If they can't do better than that, it will be a damned sight better to forget about it and use old newsreels."

I said: "You know they can't do that. This is a color picture, and on a gigantic screen."

"Well, then," he said, "they should start all over again and rethink. They should have absolute freedom of the air for the next weeks and they should do much less and much better. They should listen to advice about how it was actually fought. Then they should go up and do it so thoroughly that when people see it, they will gasp, literally gasp. They can do it if only they are told how. I saw two or three of them do low victory rolls over Duxford about ten feet up, and it was marvelous. But you have to know how to use their skill. You have to have someone—a director —who sees it with the eye of an airman, and then drives them to it."

I said: "That could be risky, couldn't it?"

"So who cares?" He was scornful. "At ten thousand feet it is terribly easy to bail out if you have to. They are refighting the Battle of Britain, and isn't that worth the risk? This is one of those films like the story of Marathon or Thermopylae—it is important—it should be approached with reverence and keenness and dedication. It must be equal to the occasion."

I said: "Have you told Guy Hamilton this?"

He shrugged. "I have only met him once. I do not know if he cares tuppence. There are too many people on this film, and you can't get to anyone. I can't go around shouting can I?"

I said: "You've just been shouting at me, and I'm listening."

"No," he said. "I cannot stand it any longer. They won't listen, I am sure of it. I am giving up. I have given in my notice. Tomorrow I leave the film."

I said: "Will you do one thing, Piotrowski. If I give you a transcript of what you've been saying, will you sign it and send it to Guy Hamilton—your complaints, your disgust, everything."

He indicated that it wouldn't do any good, but he said he would.

I shook his hand and wished him good luck on his new job. What is it, by the way?

He grinned uncomfortably. He said:

"I am going to do the drawings for the new version of *Goodbye Mr. Chips.*"

Ten days after this incident, in the course of a very close combat sequence between Spitfires and Messerschmitts, Connie Edwards turned over on his back, did a hair-raising fighter turn, and released the smoke pot on his wings which should show up on camera as a hit. As he changed his turn into a twisting dive, John Hawke in the pilot seat of the B-25 spoke over the intercom:

"I don't like to be personal, Connie, but would that be flames coming out of your engine? Aren't you being a little excessive? The script just says smoke."

There was a gasp over the intercom, and then:

"By golly, you're right. Someone's been striking matches around here. I'd better get down quick before my breeches catch fire."

The exercise was called off. The B-25 followed the two-seater Spitfire down as Edwards put it into a gentler dive and made for the fields below. The other Messerschmitts circled, the chatter of the Spanish pilots suddenly silent, and one was aware of the hypnotized stare they must be casting toward the striken plane. They had grown very fond of their Texan comrade, despite the atrocious Mexican accent he used when speaking their language.

Hawke said:

"You're doing very nicely, Connie. Why don't you cook a few enchiladas while you're on the way down? They'd do fine, the way that fire's going."

"I like steaks," Edwards said, "and moreover, I like them medium rare. That being the case, I'm going in to land now. I wouldn't like to char them."

Three miles from an emergency airfield, he put his plane down for a remarkable belly landing in a farmer's field. He lived to eat his steaks, too. By a miracle, the fire never reached the tanks and he had it practically out by the time a rescue team reached him.

A week later, at the end of nearly an hour of tricky tight flying fifteen thousand feet above the North Sea, a warning reached the squadrons from the RAF weather station. A storm was moving in on them fast, and they had better get down without delay. Hawke called the Spitfires and Messerschmitts and told them to get information behind them, and proceeded to do his shepherd act of leading them back to Debden airfield. But by the time they reached the coast, great banks of clouds had rolled in, clotted great heaps of potential thunder and turbulence.

"I can't take them through that," Hawke said to David Bracknell, the air unit director. "If something went wrong, those clouds could shred them. I've got to find a hole."

"You'd better find it fast," said Garth, the air controller. "By my calculations, the boys have only got fifteen minutes' gas left."

It was a moment when, once more, John Hawke demonstrated what he could do with his B-25. He now became not a shepherd but a sheep dog, throwing his plane around the sky in a frantic search for a way through the impenetrable clouds to the ground. Suddenly he opened up his intercom.

"Someone's been saying you drive those planes of yours like bombers," he said. "Let's see what you can really do with them. I think you've got about thirty seconds to form up behind me. Let's move!"

The sky became alive with the angry buzz of planes maneuvering into a tight formation, and then diving wing tip to wing tip upon the green and red fuselage of the Psychedelic Monster waiting ahead of them. In much less than half a minute they were on its tail and following Hawke down through a rapidly closing hole in the cloud into the murky gloom below.

Piotrowski would have been proud of the tightness of their turns and the lightning speed of their reaction. From now on, no one could accuse them of wasting time or space in the sky—or of flying their fighters like bombers.

But though the flying skill improved every time they went up, the trouble was that the weather wouldn't let them fly often enough. Each day they would turn up for the eight o'clock briefing, well knowing, for it was pouring outside, that there was not a hope of flying that day. It might not have been so bad if the pilots and the air unit crew had been back at Duxford, with a comfortable mess where they could read, play the billiard table and fruit machines, watch TV or relax while waiting for a call.

At Debden there was nothing but a drafty hangar. There the unit crew and the pilots hung around, waiting for the break in the clouds which they knew could not possibly come. The Englishmen longed for the pub, a glass of beer and a game of darts. The Spaniards ached for the comforts of the girl friends they had in the surrounding villages. Morale sagged. They lost their temper with each other. It was rather like the worst moments of a real war, when the troops have nothing to do but sit around and wait while the generals make up their minds.

To David Bracknell, the air unit director, the drooping spirits of his men was a sad thing to see, and it seemed to him that anything was better than letting them loaf around the hangar, getting bored and bad-tempered. On an obviously impossible morning he would put the briefing back until 9:30 or 10:00 a.m. And when it was over and if the weather forecast held out no hope, he would say:

"Oh, to hell with it. Let's go to the pub and have a drink."

And that was how the trouble started.

In charge of the air unit was David Haft. It was his first experience of a vile English summer, and he was not enjoying the experience at the moment. He sat in his office for hour after hour, alternately watching the sky or staring at the line of men collecting their meal trays at lunchtime.

The spectacle of those four hundred men tucking in and then coming back for more haunted him. How could they go on happily eating away in the circumstances?

"I felt like the mayor of Hamelin town," he said, "only I didn't have a Pied Piper."

The crisis came on the morning of June 21. It was about 11:30 a.m. and as Haft made his usual quarter-hourly march onto the tarmac to scan the sky, he thought he saw a patch of blue to the west. It was not big enough to make a pair of sailor's breeches, but it was enough. He dashed back to his office and sent out a call for the pilots and the crew. It was a Friday morning, the last normal working day of the week—for on Saturdays the men were paid time and a half and on Sundays they got double time. If he could only get some flying in today, at least it might stop one of those cables from New York angrily asking why he was spending so much money and getting so little film.

"But when I looked around for the boys," Haft said, "they weren't there. They were all in the pub. So I just blew up. I was so furious that the stuff started streaming out of my ears. I got hold of a runner and I told him to get over to the pub double quick. He had a simple message to deliver. It was: *Anyone who is not back here in five minutes is off this picture.* So they came pelting back, and they were up in the air in half an hour. They got some quite good stuff, too, though Bracknell maintained they would have got even better shots if they had waited a little longer. I told him in my experience a director has to take what conditions he can get. I don't think he liked that."

Bracknell, in fact, didn't like it at all. He is a tall, burly young man with blue eyes and an open face and no guile at all. While he and his crew were always intensely loyal, like many another good director, he thought of himself and his crew as "us" and the producers very much as "them" and he hated it when they interfered with his way of getting his film.

On Saturday evening, a memo. It had been written in a white-hot rage by David Haft on Friday evening and handed out to all members of the crew and all the pilots. It said:

The Battle of Britain: Aerial Unit
TO ALL CONCERNED

1. No member of this company will leave the *immediate vicinity* during business hours except in cases of emergency.

2. The local pubs are off limits for this company until after close of business for the day.

3. First morning briefings will take place at 8:00 a.m. *sharp.*

4. The weather ship will be in a standby position at all times.

5. It will fly a weather check *during* the 8:00 a.m. briefing, sending a report in by radio. A standby pilot, not involved in that particular mission, will fly this check.

6. Weather reports will be called for every thirty minutes during doubtful days.

7. Should there be the slightest possibility of a break, the weather ship will make an immediate check.

8. When the weather ship is airborne, all briefings will be complete and all flying crew will be at their airplanes to avoid any further delay.

9. Bad luck with weather notwithstanding, a lethargic attitude has invaded the unit which is unprofessional, expensive and dangerous. This operation is far too important to the picture to allow this condition to continue without comment or, if necessary, uncorrected.

David Haft
Executive Producer

" 'Ere," said one of the unit members as he read it, " 'e's treating us as if we were back in the ruddy army!"

"What's he think we are—sharecroppers?" said another.

That evening David Bracknell rang Haft at his home. "He was absolutely livid with rage," Haft recalled. "He seemed to think the memo referred specifically to him. I said, 'Hell, it's not getting at anyone in particular, but after the briefing is over there's no reason why anyone can't get up in the air in a quarter of an hour. I want pilots and crew and unit all ready to go the moment they are asked. They must be on duty. Anyone not prepared to abide by those conditions is no longer with us—and I am *not* referring to you.' But he wasn't appeased. He ranted at me for a long time. He seemed to think his boys had been insulted."

He shook his head at the memory of it. "It was a pretty nasty weekend. But it was even worse on Monday. When I walked into the hangar, I got the freeze treatment. I said, 'Good morning,' and nobody spoke to me, they all turned away. I walked over to the briefing room and everyone went silent when I came in. And over the briefing board there was a great cutout drawing of an ax pinned up. I didn't need to be told that it referred to me. I was the hatchet man on the unit. I knew they called me Ax-haft behind my back. I walked out again. It was a pretty miserable morning, I can tell you."

Finally, he called Bracknell in and said:

"Now look, when a unit is getting rotten—and this one certainly is—what it needs is somebody to hate in order to pull it back into shape again. It sort of catalyzes things. Well, now the unit's got someone to hate—me. I don't like it, but I can live with it."

Bracknell said:

"Well, we're all here, and that's what you want, isn't it?"

The freeze treatment lasted for several days, and then things began to calm down. "People began to grunt at me. They still hated me, but they were on the job and it was a very tight unit once more."

He sighed. "Don't think I didn't sympathize with them. I knew who the villain really was—the weather. But I had to find something to keep them away from the pubs. Then one day I got an idea. I was driving through a village when I saw a kid playing with one of those elastic model airplanes. I told my chauffeur to go into town and buy up as many as he could find, and he brought back boxes of them. I went round handing them out to all the pilots and the crew."

He grinned. "You know, it was marvelous. They took them into the hangar, where it was ideal for flying them. They did things to them—put holes in the wings, added flaps—so's they would loop and roll and bank. It was absolutely fantastic to see all those grown men playing around with those toys, organizing competitions, betting on them."

He added: "That reminds me. They've got a competition going this afternoon. You ought to come down and see it. Wonderful stunts you'll see. It's at three o'clock—weather permitting, of course. If the weather's fine, the competition's off."

I asked:

"Is the ax still hanging over the briefing board?"

He sighed.

"Yes," he said, sadly. And then he brightened: "But at least they don't go to the pubs anymore."

As It Was in 1940

On the night of August 25, 1940, eighty-one Hampden twin-engined bombers of the RAF took off from Bircham Newton, in southern England, on a reprisal raid against Berlin.

As the RAF chiefs had predicted, it was hardly a successful utilization of their scanty bomber force. The weather was bad. Most of the planes lost their way. Those who did reach Berlin failed to find the targets—factories and the like—which had been chosen for them, and dropped their bombs at random.

But they dropped within the confines of the German capital. Berlin had been bombed.

And, as Churchill had guessed, Hitler was lividly angry. How dare they attack Berlin? How dare they challenge him on his home ground?

He called in Göring and raved at him for an hour, and then he said:

"The British will learn to regret what they have done tonight. From now on, London is the main target. Smash it!"

So the blitz came to London. The great ordeal began for six million people as wave upon wave of Nazi bombers came up the Thames each night from now on to rain bombs upon the metropolis.

Winston Churchill did not bother to conceal his de-

Dogfight - a Messerschmitt tries desperately to evade the guns of a Spitfire.

Bombing run - in the half-light of dusk a Heinkel makes a low level attack on London.

Picketed for the night - Hurricanes dispersed on a British airfield after their last sortie of the day.

German success - a petrol bowser at Duxford is hit by a bomb and explodes.

Mission accomplished - Messerschmitt 109s return safely to their base after a raid.

Survivor - a Polish RAF pilot lands safely by parachute in Kent.

Blitz - night bombing sets the London docks ablaze.

Hurricanes

Spitfire

The Psychedelic Monster - escorted by Spitfires, John Hawke's B.25 Mitchell, the camera plane, which made it all possible.

light. With London in the firing line, Britain's plight was front-page news throughout the world. In America, pressure began to grow on the government to give the gallant Britons under siege all the aid within their power. Nazi might and tyranny must not prevail!

Air Chief Marshal Dowding was pleased for quite other reasons. He knew that the change of Luftwaffe tactics had saved the RAF from destruction and the nation from defeat.

XI

"A Dirty Little Intrigue."

On May 2, 1968, Harry Saltzman had called a conference in his Audley Square headquarters to announce the "star lineup" for *The Battle of Britain,* and the list handed to the reporters read as follows:

CAST
(in alphabetical order)

The British

HARRY ANDREWS	A senior civil servant at the Air Ministry
MICHAEL CAINE	Squadron Leader Canfield
REX HARRISON	Air Vice Marshal Keith Park, air officer commanding 11 Group
IAN MCSHANE	Andy, sergeant pilot
KENNETH MORE	Station Commander Baker
LAURENCE OLIVIER	Air Chief Marshal Sir Hugh Dowding, air officer commanding-in-chief
NIGEL PATRICK	Group Captain Hope
CHRISTOPHER PLUMMER	Squadron Leader Harvey

MICHAEL REDGRAVE	Air Vice Marshal Evill
RALPH RICHARDSON	British Minister in Bern
ROBERT SHAW	"Skipper," squadron leader
PATRICK WYMARK	Air Vice Marshal Trafford Leigh-Mallory, air officer commanding 12 Group
SUSANNAH YORKE	Section Officer Maggie Harvey

The Germans

KARL OTTO ALBERTY	Jeschonnek, chief of staff, Luftwaffe
ALEXANDER ALLERSON	Major Brandt, Heinkel bomber leader
DIETRICH FRAUBOES	Milch, inspector general, Luftwaffe
WOLF HARNISCH	General Fink
CURT JURGENS	Baron von Richter
HELMUTH KIRCHER	Foehn, fighter pilot
MALTE PETZEL	Beppo Schmidt, colonel in intelligence
MANFRED REDDEMAN	Falke, senior pilot
HEIN RIESS	Reichsmarschall Göring

It made a good deal of space in the next morning's issues of the London newspapers and got considerable international cover thereafter, but it had one mistake. Rex Harrison was *not* going to play the part of Air Vice Marshal Keith Park, and in some ways this was a pity.

The role was an important one. Keith Park was the man who had commanded the front-line squadrons of the RAF during the Battle of Britain as controller of 11 Fighter Group, whose fighters were stationed along the Channel coast between Dover and Folkestone and all the way up the Thames estuary to London. North of him were the airfields and the fighter squadrons of 12 Group under the command of Leigh-Mallory. Both of them were under the direct command of Air Chief Marshal Sir Hugh Dowding.

It was not too much to say that between Park and Leigh-Mallory there was a serious clash of personalities. Even before the battle began, they were keen rivals with different ideas on how to fight an aerial combat. Once the battle had been joined with the Luftwaffe, their differences became more pronounced. Leigh-Mallory resented the fact that Keith Park's fighters were bearing the brunt of the battle and therefore getting the major share of the glory. He longed to put his own squadrons into the air and launch them against the Germans, but by a prior arrangement was unable to do so. German aircraft operating over the precisely defined boundaries of 11 Group area were to be attacked by 11 Group fighters only. Leigh-Mallory's 12 Group fighters could only go into action over 11 Group area if and when Keith Park SOS'd for help.

In the opinion of Leigh-Mallory and his more assertive squadron commanders, this was not good enough. They were not getting their share of the action. They wanted to go in and mix it, and they deeply resented their inability to do so. On occasion fighter squadrons from 12 Group strayed into 11 Group area and shot up German fighters and bombers on their way back from raids on London and on fighter stations in the 11 Group area. Immediately there were loud cries of "Poachers!" and 12 Group fighters were told to stay out until called for. Ill feeling mounted.

Looking back on this quarrel, and upon what followed, it might seem that Leigh-Mallory and his 12 Group fighters had the argument in their favor. What did it matter which group a squadron of Spitfires belonged to so long as they shot down the Germans? On the other hand, it was a fact that 12 Group had its own area of southern and eastern England to protect, and it would have been disastrous if they had been operating in 11 Group area just when the Luftwaffe switched its attacks to their own territory.

In any case, Leigh-Mallory was not a man susceptible to such reasoning; he was headstrong and eager for glory. Moreover, he had men in his fighter wings who were desperately anxious to go in and kill Germans, and were determined to do it somehow. It was these elements who eventually persuaded Leigh-Mallory to start what were to become known as the "Big Wings." Several squadrons would take off from fields in his area and they would go out and hunt Germans and shoot them down.

This was fine, but. The only thing was that it took so long to assemble these Big Wings that they were seldom ready for action when Keith Park in 11 Group *did* SOS them for help. They arrived in time to shoot down a number of German planes, but by that time the Germans had already hit their targets—Keith Park's airfields and Keith Park's fighters. Leigh-Mallory was killing Germans, but at the cost of Britain's front-line fighters, already burning on their airfields.

Added to this, there were several occasions when 12 Group did not answer Keith Park's calls for help. They were busy on other operations. By the terms of the mandate laid down by Dowding, they were in duty bound to drop everything if 11 Group asked for their aid. But on at least two occasions—vital ones, when the Luftwaffe was coming at Keith Park's airfields in horrid strength—they failed to turn up.

In the script of *The Battle of Britain* there is a savage confrontation between the two rivals, Keith Park and Leigh-Mallory, at a crisis meeting with Dowding. It was planned as one of the dramatic moments of the film and the trio to play it had been hand-picked. Dowding would be played by Olivier, Leigh-Mallory by that artful portrayer of power-hungry types, Patrick Wymark, and Keith Park by—well, not by Rex Harrison. He had been approached not only for his professional skill but because he knew the situation well. During World War II he had been a junior officer in 11 Group under Keith Park, admired him, knew the background of his struggle.

Alas, when the weather put back shooting, his prior commitments supervened and he was forced to drop out of the cast. His place was taken by an actor of perhaps less international star quality but even more ability as an interpreter of complex roles, Trevor Howard. Still, Harrison's former association with 11 Group and Keith Park would certainly have given a sharp edge to his interpretation.

Sir Laurence Olivier was delighted when he heard of the change of cast, or so he professed.

"You know why he dropped out of the film?" he confided. "He discovered he had to do several scenes with me, and in each one of them I was his superior and he had to defer to me and call me 'sir.' He just couldn't face it!"

But neither this jocular explanation nor the simple truth, clashing dates, convinced Sir Keith Park. The former commander of 11 Group had been rewarded for his triumphs during the battle by being pushed on one side and Leigh-Mallory was the one who was given command of 11 Group; and in 1968 his sense of injustice was just as strong as when it had happened in 1940. From the moment news began to circulate about *The Battle of Britain* he had been apprehensive about the way in which he and Leigh-Mallory would be treated, and particularly anxious that the squalid facts behind the battle should not be glossed over. He carried on a lively correspondence with Air Commodore James Wallace, who was the chief liaison officer on the film, in which he sharply attacked 12 Group and its officers.

Their claims were grossly exaggerated, he said, and went on to complain bitterly about how they had continually left him in the lurch while his planes were protecting London.

The moment he learned that Rex Harrison had dropped out of the cast of *The Battle of Britain,* Sir Keith Park suspected the worst: that the hated Establishment, which had humiliated him and cast Dowding aside, was still active, still powerful, still controlling events. From New Zealand he cried "Foul!" and charged that the film was "sweeping the truth under the carpet."

A Reuter's message from Auckland was sent out at the beginning of July:

Air Vice Marshal Sir Keith Park, commander of No. 11 Fighter Group covering London and southeast England during the Battle of Britain, and now a city councillor in Auckland, has some serious doubts about the $8,000,000 film *The Battle of Britain,* now in production. He charges it will cover up "a dirty little wartime intrigue whch led to the sacking of Lord Dowding, chief of the RAF Fighter Command then."

He made the comment in Auckland last night after learning that Rex Harrison, who was to have played Sir Keith, had withdrawn from the film and been replaced by Trevor Howard.

"It is very strange that an actor taking one of the leading roles in the film should at this late hour throw in his hand. It is possible he does not agree with the script and its interpretation of the part I played in the Battle of Britain," said Sir Keith. "There was a dirty little intrigue going on behind the scenes among Air Ministry staff and the group immediately to the rear of No. 11. As a result of this intrigue, just after the Battle of Britain was won, the Air Ministry sacked Dowding, and I was sent off to a training command."

It was the worst kind of publicity, from the point of view of the producers of the film, and something obviously had to be done about it, for it would be fatal for the public to get the impression that *The Battle of Britain* was an emasculated film. Fortunately, Lord Dowding was coming to Pinewood a few days later to meet the actor who was playing him, Sir Laurence Olivier, and to see some of the rushes from the film. It was decided to enlist his aid in reassuring Keith Park.

The old man was being picked up from his home at Tunbridge Wells early in the morning and was due at Pinewood Studios at 11:00 a.m. A small delegation of people connected with the film assembled in the main entrance to greet him, Harry Saltzman, Ben Fisz, David Haft, Wing Commander Stanford-Tuck and the other air expert on the film, Ginger Lacey. Harry Saltzman was just back from New York, where he had been having urgent conferences with United Artists over the progress of the film and the state of the budget. He looked considerably thinner than when I had last seen him, but much more cheerful; for one thing, he had succeeded in having a minor operation done on his knee, which had been troubling him for some time, and he walked around happily, savoring his freedom of movement and freedom from pain.

Eleven o'clock came and went, and so did 11:15

but there was no sign of Dowding. In similar circumstances, most tycoons would have been calling for secretaries and complaining about precious time wasted, but Saltzman seemed completely relaxed and content to wait in the doorway.

"Maybe he's run out of gas," he said. "Did I ever tell you about the time Mayor La Guardia of New York was in a procession, and halfway down Fifth Avenue the car ran out of gas? Someone had forgotten to fill up beforehand."

Someone announced that a Rolls was coming through the studio gate, but when it drove up it was a new convertible Silver Shadow, and Michael Caine was in it. He had finished his part at last in Saltzman's film *Play Dirty*, which had been delayed by the rain in Almería, and was having a few days' rest before joining the cast of *The Battle of Britain*.

"A delegation—for me?" he said, as he joined the group. "I didn't know you cared."

He was introduced to Stanford-Tuck and Ginger Lacey, who proceeded to explain to him the significance of Dowding's visit. They were planning to take the old man on to the set to let him watch the confrontation scene between himself, Keith Park and Leigh-Mallory.

"Who was Keith Park?" asked Caine. "Don't forget I was a kid in those days."

Stanford-Tuck sketched in rapidly the story of Keith Park's role in the Battle of Britain.

"And who was Leigh-Mallory?" Caine then asked.

"Leigh-Mallory," said Ginger Lacey flatly, "was a clot."

Stanford-Tuck looked at him, a shocked expression on his bony features.

"Go on!" said Caine. "I thought he helped to win the Battle of Britain too."

"A clot," Ginger Lacey repeated. "I used to fly with his lot, and I know. I remember one time when he thought up an absolutely fantastic operation—he was always looking for something spectacular to draw attention to himself. This one was mad, quite mad. You hadn't a hope of coming back from it. Well, he sent his liaison officers around the squadrons explaining about the mission and asking for volunteers. But once they'd learned the details, everyone decided that it was an absolutely fatal idea, and they all decided not to volunteer. So they went back to Leigh-Mallory and told him. 'No volunteers?' he shouted. 'Why no volunteers? It shows a lamentably low standard of morale.' 'Yes,' I muttered, 'but a very high standard of intelligence.'"

Stanford-Tuck still had an expression of shock and embarrassment on his face, and he rapidly changed the subject to duck shooting.

"I'm a mad keen hunter myself," Caine said. "What do you shoot?"

"I've got a little duck shoot down on the coast," said Stanford-Tuck. "I help to cut down the deer at Cowdray in the autumn. And I get the odd shot at chamois and deer in other places now and then. What's your line?"

"Rabbits," said Caine. "I've been keen on them ever since I was evacuated to Suffolk at the beginning of the war. They used to pay us a shilling a tail for every rabbit we got. It was a wonderful way to learn to shoot." He glanced at Stanford-Tuck, and hurriedly added: "Oh, don't think we only shot rabbits, once we knew how to handle a gun. We would go off into the woods and get partridges and pheasants too."

"Whose shoot was that?" asked Lacey, with a mischievous look in his eyes.

"Gawd, I wouldn't know that," Caine said. "We was poaching, of course."

It turned out that Lord Dowding's car had broken down in Twickenham but he arrived in time to be taken straight to the theater, where the rushes were put on for him. It was a thirty-five-minute amalgam of various shots from the film which Bert Bates, the editor, had assembled. There was the sequence showing Göring's visit to his fighter squadrons; there were some beautiful shots of bombers and fighters taking off and of a nighttime scene as the squadrons of Heinkels moved up the Thames for their attack upon London; there were some short but jolting air combat scenes, and a choice confrontation between Sir Ralph Richardson, playing a British Minister, and Curt Jurgens, playing an emissary from Hitler.

These were followed, out of context so far as the film was concerned, by the first shots of Sir Laurence Olivier in the role of Dowding. I had watched it being shot and I had seen the rushes before, and it was a choice example of a great actor's skill. In real life, Olivier is something of an extrovert (though most of his admirers do not seem aware of this fact); he is gay, jokey and convivial, anxious to be liked, full of anecdotes, apt to be daringly shocking if he thinks his particular companions are the least bit squeamish or puritanical.

This was a personality exactly contrary to that of Hugh Dowding, an introvert with an in-built but invisible volcano if ever there was one. Dowding was a vegetarian, a spiritualist, a character whose lips and very being seemed to be pursed against the utterance of any indiscretion; a man whose life had been one of dedicated restraint.

It is a measure of Olivier's skill that he has not only recognized this from his researches (talks with Dowding himself, conversations with his underlings, references to the records) but was determined that his portrayal of him should not traduce the rigid spirit of the man. So this was a brilliant little gem of a scene. It is set early on in the film, before the actual Battle of Britain had begun, at the moment when France had been defeated and Britain stands alone. For six weeks the nation has been waiting for Germany to invade, and desperately trying to build up a defense against the onslaught which is coming.

The brunt of it will be born by the fighter squadrons under Dowding's command which protect the south and east coast of England. It is along these ramparts that the new radar stations have been erected to give the first warnings of enemy attacks from the air and the sea. But is Dowding ready for them? Can his fighter squadrons cope?

Churchill sends round an official from the Air Ministry to find out how Dowding is preparing. Anthony Nicholls had been picked for the part of the Minister, who was meant to be a pompous and superior type. Olivier's interpretation of Dowding during the encounter was just right. For every pressing question there was a quiet, almost inaudible answer. For every loudly expressed doubt, there was a whispered expression of confidence—and of the aloofness of a man who knows his job, wishes to be left alone to do it and despises the lofty ignorance of officialdom.

They wheeled Dowding into the theater and locked his wheelchair in place at the front of the aisle. Saltzman, Fisz, all the others had come in to watch, though they had all seen the rushes too; they were watching the real Dowding. The lights went down, the initial scenes were screened, and then the moment came when Olivier as Dowding is first seen sitting in his office at Bentley Priory as the Minister is shown in and begins his questioning of the air officer commander-in-chief.

MINISTER

The cabinet has rejected what Hitler has been pleased to call his "last appeal to reason." There's no question he's going to try it. Half the canals in Germany are blocked with barges on their way to the invasion coasts.

Two-shot. DOWDING and MINISTER. Bentley Priory. Day. Facing each other across a desk—not MINISTER's but DOWDING's.

DOWDING

We must be grateful to Herr Hitler for the six weeks' grace he has given us. Since Dunkirk, I have been able to make good nearly all the losses in France.

MINISTER

But the fact remains that against the combined enemy strength of two thousand five hundred planes, we have only six hundred fighters.

DOWDING

A few more—and God willing we will hold out.

There is a short silence.

MINISTER

Churchill puts great faith in radar.

DOWDING

It's vital. (Pause.) But it doesn't shoot down aircraft.

MINISTER

So I tell the cabinet you are trusting in radar and praying to God?

DOWDING

I'd put it the other way round. I'm trusting in God
and praying for radar.

MINISTER

But the planes they have compared with ours!

DOWDING (quietly)

Our young men will just have to shoot down their
young men at a rate of five to one.

The film faded out. The lights went up. There was
one of those horrid silences which everyone who has
ever been invited as an outsider to see the rough cut
of a film knows only too well. The men who made it
are waiting for an opinion. But slumped in his wheelchair, Dowding said nothing. Finally Ben Fisz
couldn't bear it any longer. He leaned over and said:

"What did you think of it, sir? How did you like
yourself?"

The old man said nothing for a few more seconds,
and then, in a piping voice, remarked:

"His moustache was a bit sandy, wasn't it? Was
mine really as gingery as all that?"

But now everyone was looking at him, and they
were all relaxing. They now understand why Lord
Dowding had taken so long to speak, and, knowing
what a rigidly controlled man he was, it was shattering. He was weeping.

After lunch of asparagus and omelet for Dowding,
who is a vegetarian, he was wheeled on Stage D to
meet Olivier. The actor was in the midst of one of the
most crucial scenes in the film, and it had been causing endless trouble for all concerned with it; but he at
once reacted to Dowding's presence by shrugging off
his momentary concerns and came down to explain

the scene, to introduce his fellow players, Trevor Howard and Patrick Wymark, and to demonstrate by every word and gesture the enormous admiration he had for the old man.

Presently Dowding was wheeled off to a corner with Trevor Howard so that the old man could say something to Howard about Keith Park's concern as to how he would appear on the screen; and this actor too, not always the most patient of men, bent his head deferentially and listened and faithfully promised that his portrayal would be worthy of the man worrying about his image back in New Zealand.

"A marvelous old bird!" Olivier said. "Isn't it a shame! He achieves all that, and look at the poor bleeder now, sitting in a wheelchair!"

He said it with the expression on his face of a man who has had his own confrontations with mortality and the weaknesses of the flesh, and finds them hard to bear.

Then suddenly Guy Hamilton was calling them all back to the set again, and Dowding was pushed into a corner of it, just out of camera, where he could watch. It was once more set in his office at Bentley Priory, but much later in the battle. By this time the RAF and the Luftwaffe were locked in combat, and every day there were great battles in the air over the Channel and along the Kent coast. For Keith Park and his fighters in 11 Group, the situation was grim. While his fighters were in the air defending London and Portsmouth, the Messerschmitts and Stukas were raiding his airfields along the south coast, putting great holes in his grass runways, destroying his spare fighters in their pens. He had been frantically signaling Leigh-Mallory and the fighters of 12 Group to come to his aid, and they had not come. He was bitter.

What made the scene piquant for the members of the crew was something over and above the dramatic situation and the words in the script. It was the clash of the actors involved in the scene as well as the characters they were playing. Already there had been about eight run-throughs and during each rehearsal Wymark had fluffed a line. It was beginning to fray the nerves of the other players; between attempts, Howard would stride off into the darkness beyond the lights muttering his lines, slamming his fist into his palm with tension. Olivier sat in his chair and said nothing, but every few minutes the makeup man had to come forward and wipe away the sweat coming through the greasepaint. Only Guy Hamilton seemed to remain coldly calm.

"All right," he would say, "let's try it just once again."

And then, when something went wrong once more, his face would go blank and he would say:

"Never mind. Let's relax for a moment, shall we?"

Upon which he would call Wymark over and carefully explain to him the sort of man he was playing, the reason for this confrontation between the two rivals. Wymark listened attentively, with every evidence of the confidence which seemed missing when he spoke his lines.

"It could be," someone said, "that he's so deep in his character he's got to blow his lines now and then. He certainly sounds like Leigh-Mallory when he says them. He was that sort of a man, never sure of himself."

Someone else said: "Ah, I know Wymark. You wait until Guy stops rehearsing and calls for a shot. Wymark will be word perfect. He always is. Just you see."

"I'm crossing my fingers," said one of the grips. "When we were working on *The Black Rose* in Morocco, we had thirty-five takes for one scene—and Orson Welles blew every one of them. At the end of the thirty-fifth, he just vanished out of the tent and walked off into the desert. We didn't see him again until next day. But when we did the scene, he was perfect."

As if all these thoughts had been coursing through his mind, Guy Hamilton suddenly decided that the time had come, fluffs or no fluffs.

"Now let's do it again," he said. "But this time we'll take it."

He nodded to Derek Cracknell, who went through the usual motions. In the shadows, the old man watched from his wheelchair as his screen-self leaned back behind a desk which was an exact replica of his own, and as Keith Park and Leigh-Mallory lined up in front of him.

In the scene just before an air commodore has reported to Keith Park, at a moment when news has come in of the day's devastations. His airfields have been hit again by the Germans.

"As bad as we thought, sir?" the air commodore asks.

"Worse," says Keith Park angrily. "Kenley and Biggin are a shambles again, and the rest aren't much better. God knows how many aircraft we'll have in the morning. All because 12 Group didn't do their stuff. Leigh-Mallory and his so-called Big Wing might as well stay on the ground."

It was this last sentence, during which the scene dissolved to Bentley Priory and the confrontation,

that Guy Hamilton fed to the waiting players after he
had called "Action!"

Int. DOWDING's office. Bentley Priory. Night. LEIGH-MAL-
LORY and PARK face DOWDING across his desk, which is
heavy with files. LEIGH-MALLORY is a squarely built, ambitious and forceful man, the advocate of offensive tactics.
Now he is controlled and sure of himself. PARK is trying
to appear unruffled.

> LEIGH-MALLORY (to DOWDING)
> We *were* up, sir. Trying to knock out the enemy en
> masse. But it takes time to assemble forty or fifty air-
> craft at fifteen thousand feet.

> PARK
> And by the time the Big Wing's up there, it's too
> late. The enemy have hit their targets and are on
> their way home.

DOWDING, from over his spectacles, regards his warring
commanders—reserving judgment, keeping his own coun-
sel, though his sympathies are with PARK.

> LEIGH-MALLORY (with certainty)
> Does it matter where they're shot down so long as
> they're shot down in large numbers?

> PARK
> The targets are my airfields!

> LEIGH-MALLORY
> I'd rather destroy fifty after they've hit their targets
> than ten before.

> PARK
> But you're not getting fifty. You're not even getting
> ten!

> DOWDING
> Gentlemen, you are missing the essential truth. The
> limit of our endurance is in sight. . . . We're short of

two hundred pilots. Those we have are tired and strained, and all due for relief. (Pause.) But where are the new ones?

Neither PARK nor LEIGH-MALLORY have the answer.

DOWDING

We're fighting for survival. And losing. We don't need a Big Wing or a Small Wing. We need pilots ...

In the distance we can hear the sirens starting to wail.

DOWDING

... and a miracle. ... (Pause.) Goodnight, gentlemen.

DOWDING turns to his files, as if the two COMMANDERS are already gone.

There was a long silence until Guy Hamilton softly cried: "Cut!" He was smiling with relief. There had been no fluffs, and as one watched the scene it really seemed almost unbearably real. The actors puffed out their breaths, laughed suddenly, began to chatter like magpies from sheer relaxation of tension.

I looked in the corner at the old man. For a moment he was forgotten, crouched in the shadows; and I am sure he was glad of it. If we had been riveted, what must he be feeling?

Next day Lord Dowding wrote a letter to Sir Keith Park in New Zealand, in which he felt able to say:

1 Calverley Park,
Tunbridge Wells, Kent,
July 8, 1968

My dear Park,

I have heard from indirect sources that you are apprehensive as to the way in which you will be treated by the

205

great film which is being shot on the Battle of Britain at present. . . .

. . . However as matters stand I hope that I can relieve you of any apprehensions as to the treatment you will receive at the hands of the film company. They have invited me to be present on several occasions, on their working days, and I have had the opportunity of ensuring that you will receive sympathetic treatment at their hands. Among other things I have had a talk with the actor who is going to play your part, and, although I feel sure that he would not have allowed himself to be biased in any way in his rendering of your conduct and your character, I feel sure that after what I have told him, his treatment will be actively sympathetic.

I do wish you were in England, as I feel sure that you would be invited to attend the shooting of some of the episodes and that you would be satisfied with the result.

Your sincere friend,

Dowding.

As It Was in 1940

Hitler's great gesture of revenge, the destruction of London, began on September 7, 1940.

Reichsmarschall Göring came back to northern France in his special train to supervise the onslaught. British intelligence soon heard about it, and decided that the moment for which they had waited was near at hand. The Luftwaffe was about to launch its final attack. The invasion of Britain would soon follow.

At 4:00 p.m., radar screens on the English coast picked up an unusually large number of German formations of more than twenty planes each. Messages flashed to Bentley Priory and were rushed to Dowding. He took little time to realize that this was no normal raid.

Keith Park's fighters had been readying themselves for yet another day of attacks upon their airfields, and they were taken by surprise. When Dowding sent through the news, some of them were already in the air. They waited for the German attack. It did not come. Not their way, at least.

Three hundred German bombers and a formidable protective screen of no fewer than six hundred Me-109 and Me-110 fighters roared across the Channel. But instead of pounding airfields, they made their way directly toward the Thames estuary and London.

It was a skillfully mounted attack. The Germans had learned how to be cunning in the past few weeks of battle. The bombers and fighters came in at a great height—eighteen to twenty thousand feet—and the protective escorts flew above, below and behind the bombers to give them the utmost cover.

Belatedly, the RAF fighters were scrambled and sent off to attack the invading armada. When Keith Park sent out his SOS to Leigh-Mallory this time, there was no hesitation about the response. 12 Group was more than willing to help in a clash of this kind —it was just the aggressive kind of fight for which Leigh-Mallory's boys had been waiting.

But despite repeated attacks and heavy antiaircraft fire from the ground, the Luftwaffe bombers droned on toward their target, London. And there they dropped their bombs, on oil tanks, gasworks, factories, but also on row upon row of little houses in Woolwich, Millwall, Tower Bridge, Limehouse, Tottenham, Bermondsey and West Ham.

The blitz had begun. There was death and destruction, pain and anguish, everywhere. It was the little people who were to suffer from now on.

But Dowding did not feel guilty when he looked at the devastation and heard the bombers over London and said: "Thank God." He had got his miracle and he was grateful.

On that first day, the RAF lost twenty-eight fighters. They shot down forty-one German fighters and bombers.

XII

Éminence Grise or
Big Brother?

———◆———

ALL THE TIME Guy Hamilton had been shooting at Duxford, Harry Saltzman had never once visited him on the set. One day he made an arrangement to drive out with his family so that his son could have a look at the planes, but he canceled it at the last moment.

Whenever I talked to Hamilton, I sensed a vague resentment at Saltzman's absence. Since he shared most director's views of producers—that all they think of is cutting down scenes and saving money—one might have thought that he would be glad not to have him on his back. Ben Fisz was always there, and Fisz was so dedicated to *The Battle of Britain* that he could always be relied upon to think of the film first and the expenditure second. Still, like a child who would rather have a father around to spank him than no father at all, Hamilton missed the burly man with the all-seeing eyes who asked all the awkward questions.

One night in late June I had dinner with him and his wife, Kerima, at the Bell Hotel at Lynton, in Cambridgeshire, and over a relaxing meal he unburdened himself. Kerima was dressed in a white silk trouser suit which showed off her jet black hair and gave an extra flash to her dark brown eyes.

She was obviously much concerned about her husband and felt that he was being pushed around—schedules changed to fit stars' time slots, weather worries, budget worries. I suddenly realized how tired he must be. He had been working for sixteen hours a day ever since March with hardly a break: on set every morning at eight until six in the evening, and then back home or to a hotel suite to work out the following day's shooting. Now that he had "broken the back," as he put it, of the main unit shooting, he was thinking all the time of the air sequences.

"Bracknell's getting the 'bread-and-butter shots' I need," he said. "I am the captain of this ship. I see the rushes every day. I tell him what I want and I'm determined to get what I want. But it may be that, in the end, I will have to go up in the air myself and knit it all together."

Kerima sighed.

"Still," he said, "otherwise everything's going fine. I've had a bit of trouble but on the whole, I think the star scenes are good."

He was back on his favorite subject, talking about actors. "The thing about actors," he said, "is that you try to give them running-up scenes before you get to the main scene. I've discovered that a useful way to get what I want is to tell them that this is the running-up scene and the second part is the main scene. So the running-up they do completely naturally, and the main scene they do with their full artistic fervor. Then I use the running-up scene and throw away the hammy part."

He took a sip of his wine, and Kerima leaned across and took his other hand.

"Still," he said, "I wish Harry would come round. I know some of the unit call him Big Brother, because he knows everything that's going on. But he can't *really* know until he sees it."

Harry Saltzman, in fact, was seeing things only too clearly. Every Thursday, Ron Allday, the *Battle of Britain* accountant, settled down to what he called Check Day. On that day he spent all morning and afternoon signing paychecks for actors, units and all the other personnel engaged on the film. There were so many checks that it took two suitcases to contain all of them, and it was in these suitcases that they were taken to the offices of United Artists in London for countersignature.

At the end of Check Day on Thursday, June 27, 1968, Allday went into Saltzman's office and told him that *The Battle of Britain* had spent $410,822.48 that week. The total cost of the film so far was $8,515,981.45.

"How much do we have left in the bank?" asked Saltzman.

Allday looked at his books and answered: $24,261.41. He did not need to add that, at the rate *The Battle of Britain* was spending money, that was not enough to pay for half a day's shooting.

"What are you going to do, Harry?" asked Allday.

"I'm going to New York," Saltzman said. "I'll get the money there."

Allday said: "Are you confident you're going to get it, Harry, because we've just about run out."

"What do you mean, am I confident?" said Saltzman. "I don't understand you."

211

"Well, are you going to get it?"

Saltzman: "Look, you're confusing me."

"I'm not confusing you, Harry," said Allday. "All I want to know is are you confident you're going to get this money?"

Saltzman: "Of course I am. I don't know what you're questioning me for. If I don't get it from one place, I can get it from another."

He left for New York the following morning, and three days later was back at Pinewood Studios.

"I got two million dollars," he said laconically to Allday, and they grinned at each other.

No one ever told Guy Hamilton how close *The Battle of Britain* had come to being grounded once more.

Someone on the unit defined the qualities of a successful director to me as "good strong legs, good strong bladder and infinite patience. If he has a little talent, it also helps." Watching Hamilton standing under the lowering skies at Duxford through June, July and August, waiting for a glimpse of the sun, convinced me that he possessed all three qualities in abundance; save for that blank face, deliberately drained of all feeling, you would never had guessed that he was suffering. Sometimes he swung a golf club at an imaginary ball; sometimes he walked over to a group of electricians and demonstrated how to make a penny disappear before their very eyes; and always he was prepared to discuss technique with anyone who looked interested enough to listen.

"The master shot—that's what a good film director is always afraid of," he said one morning. "It's the master shot which sets the mood of the scene, and if it goes wrong, if you let its emotions get out of con-

trol—or if you let an actor misinterpret his role in it—
you are lost, and every scene surrounding it will be
spoiled. You've got to be watching all the time. You
read the script and the scene looks and sounds all
right; then in comes the star and, if you aren't careful,
wrecks the whole thing."

Susannah York came over to join us. She played the
part of an officer in the Woman's Auxiliary Air Force
at a fighter station during the battle. Even in her World
War II uniform she looked disturbingly pretty. To a
modern eye, the blue WAAF uniform of 1940 was not
exactly attractive: a round hat, shaped rather like a
half-collapsed soufflé, worn flat on the head, a
square-shouldered and belted jacket, a skirt down to
midcalf, gunmetal thick stockings and sensible black
shoes. Most of the extras playing WAAFs in *The Battle of Britain* rolled up their skirts between shots to
show that they still had thighs, and the shapely
blonde who acted as Susannah York's stand-in slipped
hers off and substituted a microskirt which was barely
visible below her jacket.

York managed to remain touchingly attractive without doing anything to her costume at all. One was
never for a moment unaware that there was a woman
underneath all that clobber.

"Some actresses can read the telephone book and
make it sound dramatic," said Derek Cracknell, "and
some can wear a sack and still look sensual."

But that York could also act and feel we soon had
no doubt. She had come across to Hamilton to discuss
her next scene with him and one could sense at once
that he was going to have no trouble with her. She
listened attentively to every word he said, and
watched in dead earnest as he acted out in front of

213

her the movements and the expressions he was hoping to get from her. She walked off for a moment, saying: "Do you mind if I just think this out for a moment?" and we left her, pacing up and down, her rose pink face wearing an expression of delicious concentration.

I remarked to Hamilton that it must be gratifying to have a star who really listened and tried to understand what a director was seeking. He nodded.

"She's a wise girl. She doesn't mind a kick up her pretty rump now and then. She can get very kittenish on screen, and she knows it. She likes to be told when she's doing it."

Presently she rejoined us.

"I think I've got it now," she said. "I'd like to try it."

She was very serious, no hint of laughter left on a face which, normally, was as cheerful as a child's.

It was a good scene for her, and she knew it. The part of Maggie in the film is that of a young girl, recently married to a Battle of Britain pilot (Christopher Plummer), who slowly becomes involved in the war and her part in it. She commands a company of WAAFs on one of the front-line fighter stations (but not that of her husband) at a moment when it is under heavy attack from the Luftwaffe. Until that moment her knowledge of what war can mean has been only vicarious; true, some of the pilots from the station don't come back from their missions, but so long as her husband is safe, the impact is bearable.

But then comes the day when the station is heavily and devastatingly bombed. She stops being an onlooker and becomes a participant instead.

They had shot the bombing of the airfield and the hangars the day before, and now came the aftermath.

Smoke still rises from the burning buildings. Huge craters pit the airfield. There has been a direct hit on one of the slit trenches where the WAAFs—*her* WAAFs—have been sheltering. Now the bodies have been brought out and laid on the grass, blankets over them, their legs sticking out, still covered with gunmetal stockings and sensible shoes.

We waited for the sun to make an appearance through the heavy clouds, and then Freddie Young took his dark lens from his eye and said:

"Okay, if we're quick."

Hamilton looked across at York, who was standing over the bodies, looking down.

"You ready, Susannah?"

She gave just the faintest nod by way of reply.

"Right. Action!"

Exterior. Station "B." Day. The raid is over and there is a terrible expanse of wreckage. The hangars are still blazing, and heavy acrid smoke hangs like a pall over the scene.

In F.G. a lorry full of "walking wounded" WAAFs is preparing to leave under MAGGIE's supervision. Though none is seriously hurt, they are a pitiful sight—dirty, disheveled and, in some cases, bandaged. Shock is setting in and a very young GIRL is sobbing quietly.

MAGGIE approaches the tailboard with WAAF Corporal SEYMOUR and another WAAF with a bandaged head. MAGGIE and SEYMOUR help her in. The young GIRL sobs on.

MAGGIE (sharply)

Bates—pull yourself together! (To SEYMOUR) Better go with them, Seymour.

SEYMOUR—a brisk and capable woman—hesitates.

MAGGIE

That's all right. I'll see to it.

SEYMOUR climbs into the lorry as MAGGIE turns, and walks toward the debris.

Exterior. WAAF trench. Day. Beside the mounds of scattered earth, eight corpses, each roughly covered with a blanket. The odd protruding leg-shoe-ankle tells us that this WAAF trench has suffered a direct hit.

MAGGIE stands and looks. She begins to shake violently. Trying to control herself, she reaches in her gas mask and takes out a packet of cigarettes with trembling hands. She puts a cigarette in her mouth and is fumbling for her lighter when . . .

VOICE (screams, offscreen)

Put that cigarette out!

We see that it is an RAF warrant officer, WARRICK. He is in charge of a party of AIRMEN towing away wreckage.

Warrick (yells)

The mains have gone! Can't you smell gas, you silly bitch!

This is the last straw. MAGGIE begins to crumble. She stares at WARRICK with hot, tear-filled eyes. But he's already forgotten about it. MAGGIE finds the will to reassert herself.

MAGGIE

Don't you yell at me, *Mister* Warrick!

WARRICK turns and stares at her, bewildered. Then carries on with his work. He will never know how much he has helped her.

The first time she went through the scene, York opened her mouth to shout: "Don't you yell at me!" and no sound came out. Tears coursed down her cheeks instead. She wiped them away angrily.

"Sorry," she said.

"That's all right," Hamilton said softly. "Don't worry. Take your time."

We all realized that this was really happening to her now, that those were real dead bodies at her feet, that this was the end of a terrible day.

She walked off and paced up and down, swallowing hard, taking deep breaths.

"I'm all right now," she said. "I can do it now."

Hamilton said: "In that case, we'll shoot it."

Shoot it they did, three times in all, but not because Susannah York fluffed her lines again, but because Hamilton obviously sensed, as we all did, that each time it would get better. She gave the scene intense feeling and emotion, and not only was she weeping copiously by the end but all of us had tears in our eyes too.

"Cut! All right, let's break for lunch," shouted Hamilton. At once York turned on her heel and walked away, alone. No one applauded her as she went off, but you felt that everyone would have liked to have done so.

Half an hour later, in the bar of the mess across the road, she joined us for a drink before lunch. The grime of the bombing sequence makeup had disappeared; she had changed into a miniskirt with a tiny denim jacket and a bare midriff, and she had sandals on her feet; she looked as pink and scrubbed as a newly bathed baby, although paternal feelings were by no means those felt by all who watched at her.

When she began to talk, however, you realized that she was still under the influence of the scene she had been playing that morning.

"It seems funny now," she said, "to remember that when they first asked me to play in this film, I wanted to turn it down. I would have done too if it hadn't been for the money. I said to myself: The Battle of Britain, oh God, what a bore. All those people talking that strange jargon and all those boring airplanes. Anyway, I'm antiwar. And honestly, really, I didn't know anything about the Battle of Britain at all—knew more about the Battle of Hastings, in fact. At least I'd read about that at school."

She sipped her gin and tonic reflectively.

"Then one day on the set at Pinewood I was introduced to Bill Foxley and told I was going to do one of my scenes with him. Do you know Bill Foxley?"

Yes, I said, I knew Bill Foxley. He was a Battle of Britain pilot who had been shot down and badly burned about the face and hands. He belonged to the Guinea Pigs Club, the association of burned pilots, and he had been brought in to do a scene in a RAF plotting sequence—because damaged and grounded pilots were often used in this way.

"It was the first time I had ever come really close to a man who has had his face burned," York said, "and I knew there was one thing I mustn't, mustn't do, and that was not look him straight in the eye. So I did that. He held out his hand and I took it. And that was the moment, I think, when something changed gear in me. I hadn't realized that his hands had been so badly burned. I only heard afterward about how Battle of Britain pilots used to take their gloves off to get better control of their planes, and then—when the fire started—they . . ." She gulped. "Am I sounding like an awful, childish, innocent bloody fool?" she asked.

"Anyway . . . I took his hand and I realized what the whole ordeal must have been like. And then, each

218

time we met after that, he would still hold out that deformed hand, and I would still take it, I would still look him straight in the face, and suddenly—well, suddenly he wasn't a man who was burned any more, but the nice man he is under the skin. We were suddenly in communication, and it wasn't just between a man and a woman, but between a different generation, a different kind of experience."

She paused and then added: "That's when I got hooked on *The Battle of Britain*. I not only wanted to play in it. I wanted to know all about it, too."

Next day, at Pinewood, she did a bedroom scene with Christopher Plummer, and it was hard to believe she was the same girl. They cleared the set of all but the most essential personnel, for she first had to move around a hotel bedroom in a WAAF shirt, stockings and suspender belt, and then take them off to climb into bed with her eager but resentful husband.

While the cameras were on her, she was the sauciest girl you have ever seen, pretending to be shy but deliberately flaunting her sensual attractions against the craggy dialogue which was going on between the two players—for he wanted her to give up her job, she wanted to stay on it.

But once the scene was through and the lights were doused, she relaxed as if shirt and suspender belt were just another form of bikini bathing suit, which, in fact, they are not. Lounged back, smoked a cigarette, didn't care. It was just the right attitude, too. The unit took their cue from her. There was no denying their almost Peeping Tom intensity while the scene was in progress, and no mistaking their complete aloofness once it was over.

The bombing of Duxford airfield was the biggest and most expensive blowup in the film. The unit called it the Last Blow, although there would, in fact, be a big dockside spectacular toward the end of the shooting schedule. But this one was by far the most complicated and its preparations had certainly caused the most trouble. The sequence was to be a series of multiple explosions—to simulate a stick of German bombs—dropping across the airfield, over the tarmac (and onto the WAAF slit trench), and ending with a direct hit on one of the three huge hangars on the edge of the field. The hangar was about sixty yards wide, two hundred yards long and a hundred feet high and had been built by the RAF to last. It would need a gigantic amount of explosives to blow it down.

When the film company had hired the airfield from the British Ministry of Defense, it had been assumed that permission to destroy the building had been given. It had certainly been mentioned in conversation. But when the production manager, John Palmer, looked into the agreements, he had an unpleasant surprise.

INTEROFFICE MEMORANDUM

FROM: John Palmer

TO: Mr. David Haft
copies to Messrs.
Saltzman, Fisz
May 28, 1968

SUBJECT: LOCATION DUXFORD—Station "B"
Scenes 152 to 164 (bombing)

Following a discussion with Maurice Carter at North Weald today, I would like to make, with your help, absolutely certain that we are covered from every point of view when we commence the bombing sequence on the hangar at Duxford.

Apart from Defense Land Agent (Ministry of Defense) License NKT/31/93/LA.2 see pp. 4 & 5 dated May

7, 1968, granting us permission to use RAF Duxford airfield as a location, I have not seen any specific document giving us permission to destroy certain parts of hangar no. 3.

I believe it is Maurice Carter's considered opinion that we may possibly cause more damage to the hangar during our simulated explosion sequence than may have been envisaged during the planning stages.

Whereas both Cliff Richardson and Glen Robinson and their teams are fully qualified special-effects experts, it occurs to me that it would be advisable to examine the possibility of consulting with an independent body of explosive experts to afford us additional backup.

I am particularly anxious to have sight of our Ministry of Defense permits for this sequence and at the same time do not wish to open a can of beans.

May I hear from you please?

John Palmer

He heard, instead, from Ben Fisz, who consulted the documents and discovered that there was, in fact, no specific permission to destroy the hangar.

"It can't be done," he said. "It will cause too much damage and cost too much money to replace. We abandon it and use other methods instead."

He paused, and then added: "But don't let's tell Guy about this. Not yet, anyway. He will be very disappointed."

He was understating Hamilton's reaction. The director was relying a great deal on the authenticity of the bombing of Duxford airfield and the destruction of the hangar in order to lead in to his scene with Susannah York and the dead WAAFs. Since you can never keep a secret on a film set, news of the producer's decision reached him within an hour or two, and he was furious.

He stormed into Fisz's office and said.

"I must have my explosion! I've got to have it!"

Fisz smiled at him, like a father denying a child a box of matches.

"I know just how you feel, my dear," he said. "It is a great pity. But the explosion is too big—too dangerous—too expensive."

He got up and put his arm round Hamilton. "But don't worry. We'll work up something that will look just as effective."

The director vehemently shook his head. "You'll ruin the whole sequence," he said. "If the explosion looks phony, Susannah's scene will look phony, and that will spoil everything. I want my explosion. I'm going to have my explosion! I'm going to see Harry about it."

"Look," said Saltzman to Fisz that night, "if Guy wants his explosion, you'd better give it to him."

Said Fisz: "But what about the permissions and the damage and the cost?"

"We'll work that out when the time comes," said Saltzman. "Give him his explosion."

So the word had gone out to the death-and-destruction team that the hangar was to be well and truly destroyed. *"Blow now, pay later* is the watchword," said Maurice Carter.

There is something about a big explosion or a fireworks display that brings out the small boy in everyone, including women, and on June 21 all the wives came to see the Big Blow. Kerima was there, tall, slim, elegant in a dark trouser suit, her face lit up and her eyes bright with excitement. She said she was nervous.

"I always worry for Guy at times like this," she said. "So many things can go wrong."

"He'll be safe enough behind that," said Susannah

222

York, pointing to the wooden screens with slit holes in them which had been built to protect the crew and the cameras.

Kerima shook her head. "Not wrong in that sense. He can take care of himself. I mean if the scene goes wrong, if the explosives fail or only half go off. What then? They can hardly do it again."

They began to talk about filming, and York said how hard it was sometimes, especially if you believed in your part, not to get too worked up about it. Kerima laughed.

"I was once making a film in Paris," she said, "where I was a young wife and my husband is supposed to come back to me after being away for five years. He is very much in love with me and takes me in his arms. So this actor who is playing my husband, he comes into the room and he grabs me, and—nothing!" She lifted her hands and her dark eyes skyward and shrugged. "So the director, he says, 'When you take her in your arms, you must show passion, you must give to her, show how you've been longing for her.' The actor grabs me again, and again it is nothing—nothing—nothing!"

She laughed again as she saw us looking at her in disbelief. "Is true," she said. "So then the director takes me on one side and says, 'I must have this scene right. You must make him do it right. Do anything to him—burn him, kiss him, anything. I want to see this man feel something.' Well, it takes me a long time, you know. I have to work a long time. This man is like an ice cube. I have to work and work and *work!* And finally, finally we shoot the scene. And do you know what?" She was bubbling with mischievous laughter now, her dark hair and her shoulders shaking. "He was no good anymore! He was no *good* anymore! He was not the one who had come up, he was the one who was going down. And I—I was the one who was up!"

Kenneth More came over to join us. "God, I have a terrible time remembering names and people these days," he said. "That chap over there, for instance, I've just been talking to. Sure I've met him before some time. A photographer or something. Don't like to be rude to the press, but who the hell is he?"

"My husband," said Susannah York.

"What did I tell you?" said More. "Just can't remember people any longer."

The extras were moving into their places now and complicated instructions were being passed over the walkie-talkies. Derek Cracknell took up his bullhorn.

"Will all those people who are not in this scene and are not on the cameras please move back," he said. "Well back. If you've got tin hats, wear them. If you haven't, keep your heads down."

We walked across the field and Kerima, as if she felt she must talk, talk, talk, just to cover her nervousness, said:

"Stars think they are so important. Once when I started making films, I thought all the good things on the screen came from the inspiration of the artist, and that the directors and the technicians had nothing to do with it. And then I learned—darling, I learned! I realize now you don't need stars except for their names. You can make films with puppets."

We took refuge behind a substantial bulldozer some way down the field.

"Stars can be so naughty—vicious even," she said. "Especially the men—and especially to the women

who have to play with them. I once played with
. . . " she mentioned the name of a famous international star—"who was always coming behind me,
especially in my close-ups, and trying to steal my
scenes. In one close-up, I could feel him touching my
hair, and I stopped the scene and said: 'You're dis-
turbing my wig. You mustn't come so close to my
hair. Stay out of my scene.' But when we tried it
again, I could feel him moving my hair again, and I
was so mad I threw back my hair in his face just at
the moment when he was trying to get in camera. He
was furious, *furious*. And you know what? Later on,
there was a scene where he had to slap me and throw
me on to the bed. Then we fight. Well, he slapped me
so hard that he knocked me six feet across the room,
and I crashed against the corner of the bed. Woof! I
couldn't walk for a week, and there he was, looking
down at me, with an expression in his eyes like:
'That'll show you, you terrible woman!' Oh, they can
be so naughty, these male stars!"

Derek Cracknell was on the bullhorn again. "All
right, everybody. Places! We're ready to go."

Like a crowd waiting for a brick to be thrown
through a plate-glass window, we tensed into silence.
I could feel Kerima's fingers gripping my sleeve.

Then it began. A burst of flame and a mushroom-
shaped cloud of smoke rose from a collapsing hut on
the other side of the field, followed seconds later by
another and another and another bursting, a hundred
yards apart, in a line leading straight toward the
great hangar.

"Here it comes," I said. "The big one."

But when the last explosion burst against the side
of the hangar, something went wrong. A hole was

torn out of the side, but the building stayed erect.
You would never have guessed that there was half a
ton of gelignite and three tankers of oil inside, waiting to be ignited.

"Oh God," said Kerima.

"I'm sorry," I said.

"Oh God," she said again.

But that day *The Battle of Britain* was lucky. It
was assumed that the sequence was ruined, that there
was no hope of repeating the bombing; but the producers reckoned without the determination of the two
explosives experts, Richardson and Robinson. Five
minutes after the failure, and despite the risk that the
gelignite might go off inside by delayed action, they
were inside the hangar, tinkering with the fuses. They
emerged grimy and sweaty, but triumphant.

"We can do it again," they said. "And this time
we'll pack another half a ton of explosives inside, just
to make sure."

And next day, the hangar went up in the most spectacular eruption of smoke and flame that even veterans of the blitz can remember.

Kerima was not there to see it. She just couldn't
stand the ordeal twice, she said.

The moment the smoke and dust began to clear,
and the debris stopped raining down, Derek Cracknell called out through the bullhorn:

"All right, everyone, first places! Let's not break up
the mood. Let's do it just once more."

It took everyone, including the crew, several seconds to realize that he was joking, and that the giant
hangar didn't exist anymore.

As It Was in 1940

By switching the Luftwaffe's attack to London, Herman Göring brought relief to the RAF at the most critical moment of the Battle of Britain. Not until after World War II was over could it be revealed how close Keith Park's 11 Group fighters had come to being put out of action. In the previous ten days, British losses had been well-nigh catastrophic. The pilots in their Hurricanes and Spitfires continued to shoot down more of the enemy than they lost themselves, but sometimes the figures were very close. On the worst day, Saturday, August 31, for instance, the RAF lost thirty-nine aircraft and fourteen of their pilots were killed. They shot down forty-one Luftwaffe fighters and bombers.

In view of the fact that the Germans still had a superiority over the British of four to one, that was an appallingly bad day.

Now the tide turned. Not only did the change of tactics give a respite to 11 Group; it also made the Luftwaffe far more vulnerable. With the target changed to London, the Me-109s escorting the German bomber fleets suddenly found themselves overstretched. They had fuel enough to get them to London and back, but not enough to allow them to stay over the target for any length of time or to maneuver as they wished during an air battle. Many a German pilot now had to fight for his life all the way up and down the Thames and then, if he was lucky, would be forced to glide home across the Channel on an empty tank. Wrecked German aircraft began to pile up on the beaches around Cape Gris-Nez.

Night and day the German bombs rained down upon the people of London and Liverpool and other great cities, and the suffering was great. But the killed, the maimed, the homeless and the nerve-racked were suffering in a good cause. Just by being the target for the enemy they were winning the war.

In Berlin Adolf Hitler waited for news that the RAF was collapsing and that the people were cracking under the strain of the blitz. Then he would invade. The troops were all now poised and ready.

"Give me five more days," Göring told him. He had asked for five days at the beginning of the battle, and that was more than a month ago. But now Hitler consented to give him yet five more.

On September 14 the RAF shot down only fourteen German planes, and Göring was overjoyed. He rushed to telephone Hitler, who ordered the invasion troops to stand by. The hour of destiny was at hand.

XIII
Rough Cut

———————◆———————

IT IS A strange feeling inside a film unit when its members begin to realize that an epic is approaching its end. Ever since early March, and it was now September, hundreds of men and women had been thinking of nothing but the critical problems of *The Battle of Britain*. Suddenly they became aware once more of their own, and began to give them priority. What would they do next? For the less important members, there was a certain tension as they looked inside their pay slips on Friday night: would there be a two-week notice alongside their pay slip? For the chief technicians, there was the restiveness of men and women who have already been approached for other films, and wonder which is the best psychological moment to get out.

So far as the hard core of the unit was concerned, work would go on for months to come, of course.

It was a time when one's admiration for Ben Fisz, the man who had been on the spot from the beginning, mounted. He had been living with this film for more than three years now and every crisis it had experienced and weathered had never been, so far as he was concerned, the normal hazards which most big films go through. *The Battle of Britain* was still his baby. He had conceived it and nursed it through its early setbacks, its teething troubles, its almost fatal beginnings.

Now that the film had taken shape and most of the great disasters had been overcome, you might have thought that he would relax. Several times Harry Saltzman urged him to go off and "get a little sunshine." But so long as there was still work to be done on location, so long as a camera was turning, he was there to watch it, to see that all went well, to take the vital decisions which are forced upon a producer every day and only he can answer: *It's raining again and the forecast is lousy. Do we work overtime this weekend—and risk paying the crew double pay for a workless Sunday?* Or: *If we get out of this airfield in the next three days, we can save $19,000. We can do it if the crew, the weather and the actors behave. But what if they don't? We've got to make the decision by noon today. What do we decide?*

Always problems, problems, problems. A producer's life on a normal film is a constant worry, a constant fight against time, money and temperament. But *The Battle of Britain* contained imponderables no other film has ever faced, colossal and costly. Added to which Fisz knew that if he decided wrong, it was not any ordinary film which would be injured. It was his own cherished epic for which he had fought and bled.

The surprising thing was how cool, calm and friendly he kept his outside demeanor when you realized what anxieties must be burning inside. He was up at five each morning to work in his office in London, and then out to the airfield in Cambridgeshire to spend the whole day on the set or on the telephone or in conference with Guy Hamilton (often in a windblown hangar sheltering from the rain). Then back to work on the next day's shooting until long after midnight. He was a tough man and yet a sensitive one, defying weariness because of a burning determination to see his film through and make it a success.

Guy Hamilton too would be on the film until the end, and so would his cameraman, Freddie Young, and his assistant, Derek Cracknell,* and his art director, Maurice Carter. For the publicity department under Derek Coyte the real chores of selling the film to the world were now approaching, and hard facts and good stories would be more important now than trim assistants in miniskirts.

Even the stars were beginning to depart. Robert Shaw and Christopher Plummer took off for Peru to play two very different kinds of warriors, the Spanish and Aztec protagonists in *The Royal Hunt of the Sun*. Susannah York did her last emotional scene and then departed for America to play a very different role from the WAAF section leader in *The Battle of Britain;* she was going to be the drab Lesbian slut in *The Killing of Sister George*.

"Do you think they picked me for the part because I have such a boyish figure?" she asked, displaying her pink tummy in yet another midriff suit.

We all solemnly assured her that she would always be heterosexual to us, and she left amid a damp and tearful sequence of emotional farewells, not least with the man with the war-scarred hands, Bill Foxley.

---

* Though Stanley Kubrick was already seeking Cracknell, his "favorite" assistant on *2001*, to join him on his next film.

Toward the end of August a small group of Spitfires and Messerschmitts, plus the Psychedelic Monster, flew across France to Montpellier, on the Mediterranean, in search of some sunshine to complete a sequence of aerial combat shots. They had a perilous journey on the way down through sleet, hail and fog, and the sunshine they found at the end of the journey was accompanied by a mistral which blew so hard that they could not take off for two days. Finally, they limped their way back to Duxford.

There were increasingly anguished cries of pain from New York now from United Artists about the size of the budget on *The Battle of Britain*. Everyone had long since accepted the fact that the price of the film was bound to be over $10,000,000, which was the figure which had been accepted after Harry Saltzman's last visit to New York.

But how much more?

I was in Saltzman's office one afternoon in London when he spoke to New York.

"We'll bring it in at $11,600,000," he said. "Don't worry, that will be the final figure. It's only the weather for the flying sequences which is holding us up."

When he put down the telephone, he said to David Haft:

"Jeez, we've got to get rid of those planes. It's the planes that are costing us all this money."

Haft said: "You can't get rid of the planes until we've got all the shots Guy needs."

Saltzman said: "What shots does Guy need?"

Haft said: "You'll have to ask Guy. And maybe he won't tell you, either."

Just before September 15, 1968, which was Battle

of Britain Day, General Adolf Galland came to London once more. He and a small group of Luftwaffe pilots from World War II had been invited to the International Air Show by the Pathfinders' Association, an elite group of RAF bomber pilots of whom Group Captain Hamish Mahaddie was a leading member. But though it was an honor they appreciated, Galland and his fellow fighter pilots wanted something more —a meeting with veteran fighter pilots of the RAF against whom they had fought in the Battle of Britain, and a visit together to the Spitfires and Messerschmitts at Duxford.

The approach was made to Ben Fisz, who at once concealed his alarm behind a most sympathetic smile.

"What a wonderful idea!" he said. "I am all for it. Providing," he added, "that the Battle of Britain Association's members agree. They will have to be asked."

"Please ask them," said Galland.

"I will, I will," Fisz assured him.

But the moment Galland had left, the dire possibilities of the idea danced before his mind's eye. He knew only too well that, though twenty-eight years had passed, there were plenty of Battle of Britain pilots who would not be seen in the same room as a flier in Hitler's Luftwaffe. Nevertheless, he picked up the telephone and called Group Captain Tom Gleave, who is one of the Battle of Britain Fighter Association's most prominent members. He promised to put the proposal to his fellows at their general meeting just before their annual celebration dinner on September 15.

A small group of people associated with *The Battle of Britain* had been invited to attend the dinner that night, and as they came into the anteroom of Bentley

Priory, Ben Fisz espied Tom Gleave and went over to him.

"How did it go?" he asked.

Gleave, who was badly burned in the battle but bears no man a grudge, looked glum. He pointed toward Douglas Bader, who was moving around among his comrades and gleefully shouting:

"We won, we won!"

It turned out that none of the RAF veterans was really against the project to meet their erstwhile German enemies at Duxford until two speeches were made. They were highly emotional. They claimed that twenty-eight years was too soon to forgive and forget, and that the widows and children of men killed by the Luftwaffe in 1940 would be shocked if RAF pilots were seen to be carousing with their murderers in 1968.

"So the project was voted down. Ninety-five to five. You can tell them they can't come," Gleave said.

When he heard of the decision, Galland was devastated. "How can they go on bearing these grudges?" he asked. "It was a fair war up there in the air. We were all equal. We asked no favors—and we had no politics. Why can't they realize that?"

He was now sporting a Pathfinder tie. But what was that compared with an invitation from the fighter pilots against whom he had fought during the battle?

Ben Fisz said: "In a way, I'm glad it didn't happen. You know what pilots are like. They drink hard and they make remarks. By the end of the visit, I'm sure we'd have had one of the British pilots calling one of the German pilots a Kraut or a Nazi, and then someone would have got punched in the nose. That wouldn't have been nice, would it?"

"It would have been splendid publicity," I said.

"Ah, yes," said Fisz, and sighed.

By the second week in September 1968, warning flags were flying over Pinewood Studios. There were rumors of financial pressure again and a rapidly diminishing budget. Practically all but a few minor scenes with the stars had been completed now, and Guy Hamilton had left for Duxford to knit together the flying sequences—as everyone always had believed he would. But the drain on the company's resources from the flying unit was still appallingly high, and Saltzman was grateful to Rank Films for a munificent gesture. The *Battle of Britain* company owed them a large sum in rental and labor costs, and the bill was now due. Rank offered to wait for payment—and this gave Saltzman an extra $600,000 to juggle with just when the company most needed it.

But both he and his accountant knew that an extra $600,000 would by no means see them through, and that soon United Artists would have to be asked to raise the budget again.

It was an illuminating experience to observe Saltzman in operation during this critical period. While watching over the destiny of *The Battle of Britain* he was also getting several other films into action—a new James Bond film for which, at that time, he was still searching for a new actor to play James Bond; a science-fiction musical; a *comédie noire* about a modern Jesus to be shot in France by Luis Bunuel; a film about the life of Karl Marx's daughter Tussy; a Zola novel he wanted to screen with Simone Signoret and Jeanne Moreau; and the life of Nijinsky with Nureyev. Whenever you met him, he was just off to Madrid or Rome or Zurich, or just back from Paris or

Munich or Cologne. He had learned to love traveling by air in the 1930s, when his theater agency got free tickets from the air companies for advertising them in their theaters; but even a man as hooked on flying as he was must have wearied of it sometime. He showed no signs of it. The only time he seemed to lose his temper was with agents, toward whom he seemed to have a phobia, but otherwise he was equable in the extreme. He let his underlings argue with him and shout at him and bore it patiently, even when they were manifestly wrong or merely trying to demonstrate to outsiders that he didn't overawe them.

One afternoon he came into his Audley Street office for an hour of conferences. He had spent the morning in Paris and would be off to Rome by the afternoon plane.

"I've got to change my trousers," he said, slipping them off as he spoke. "Someone spilled coffee on them on the way over." To a secretary, "Get me another pair of pants."

At this moment, a dazzling young woman came into the room; she was a very tall, leggy colored girl who had been sent for his inspection for a role as one of 007's girls in the new Bond film. Beyond no doubt she was a charmer, and Saltzman was aware of it. He got up to greet her, and neither she nor he seemed to be conscious of the fact that while they were talking he was walking around in his jacket, a flapping shirt and no trousers.

He was accompanying the girl to the door at the end of the interview when it opened, and in came his wife, Jackie, and his young son. After the girl had gone, Mrs. Saltzman said:

"I didn't like the way you were looking at that woman."

The boy took his mother's hand and said loyally:

"Don't worry, mom, she was too tall, and she was ugly, too."

Jackie looked at her husband, and then both of them began to laugh.

On September 23, David and Arnold Picker flew into London. They were the heads of United Artists and they had come to England to see for themselves what sort of a film it was that was taking so long, causing so much trouble and costing so much money.

Guy Hamilton was called in from Duxford and he and his cutter, Bert Bates, set to work to finish a rough cut of the film for showing to the American executives. The performance was set for 2:00 in the afternoon, and at ten seconds before that time the Pickers walked in and Arnold said:

"Let's go."

For the next two and a quarter hours they sat and watched in complete silence. The others there were Saltzman, Ben Fisz, Guy Hamilton, Derek Coyte, David Haft and Saltzman's New York lawyer. They didn't utter, either.

The rough cut was a splendid example of Hamilton's professionalism. Almost all of the film was now stitched together and many of the scenes on the ground were superbly done, the confrontations emotional in the extreme, the blitz scenes and the bombing sequences colorfully spectacular. No one could grumble about the air scenes, either, except that they had gaps in them which Hamilton was now busily filling in. For the moment, to keep the continuity of the rough cut going for the Pickers, he cunningly let the screen go blank and then superimposed his own voice, explaining just what would be happening here.

"This is where we cut away from Harvey struggling in the cockpit, trying to get out," he would say, "and show his parachute opening and his drop down into the Channel." Or: "The next shot you will see is Falke's brother bleeding in his plane as it goes down in a steep dive. This blank space you're looking at now is the scene I'm shooting at the moment of Falke getting it in the back from a Spitfire."

Finally it was over and the lights went up. The Pickers said nothing, Arnold turned to Saltzman and once more said:

"Let's go."

The party then drove away from Pinewood in a procession of cars to Saltzman's house, Woodlands Park, some ten minutes away. It is an estate to make a film star living in Bel Air green with envy. There is a vast paddock in which the family ride on weekends, a home farm which supplies their milk, cream and butter, a lovingly tended park full of massive oaks, and an ornamental lake. The house is huge and airy, with a great open terrace, and on the second floor is a twenty-five-yard-long swimming pool with air conditioning and floodlights for night bathing parties.

It was here, in the lounge, that what was laughingly called afternoon tea was served to the visitors. A great table groaned under every kind of sandwich, sausage, hors d'oeuvre and sweetmeat. Jackie Saltzman and her sister moved around, urging the guests to eat. The Pickers politely waved the food away on the grounds that they were dieting. They sipped tea, as did Saltzman. Most of the others were nervously drinking gin-and-tonics or vodka.

It was noticeable that the two United Artists chiefs spoke to no one except Saltzman. There were no words with Hamilton or with Fisz. And still no word was said about the film. Finally, Arnold Picker said:

"Let's go and have a talk, shall we?"

Saltzman rose, as did his lawyer, and the two of them led the Pickers across the room to his study. The others stayed behind, beside the groaning table of food, waiting. They waited a long time. When Saltzman emerged again, the Pickers had gone.

"I'm going to New York in the morning," he said.

Nobody dared to ask him what the Pickers had thought about the film. It must have been a miserable moment in Guy Hamilton's life.

It was Friday when Harry Saltzman took off for New York, and Ron Allday, the *Battle of Britain* accountant, was worried. He knew that Saltzman had to be in Switzerland for a conference about the Bond film on Saturday evening. On Saturday afternoon he had a duty which, Allday was sure, he would not want to miss. It was Fete Day in Iver Village, where Woodlands Park was situated, and Saltzman was proud of being squire of the village and a member of the community. He would want to be there. He had accepted the task of picking from out of the local aspirants a young girl from the village as queen of the fete.

In which case, when would he have time for a meeting with his accountants? That there would have to be a meeting was certain and urgent. The pennies were dribbling away again. Would there be enough left in the kitty to pay wages next Check Day?

In the early hours of Saturday morning, Allday was awakened by the telephone. It was the post office with a cable from New York. Saltzman was on his way home.

"He asked me to be ready for a meeting an hour after he touched down," Allday said. "That just gave him time to go home to Woodlands, have a bath and change, and drive out to our rendezvous. Do I have to tell you where it was? At the Iver Fete. Harry went round being nice to the locals and choosing the girl who would be queen of the fete. In the meantime, he talked business with us. I've had some strange meetings in my time, but this was the queerest. He would go off to chat to some schoolteacher or councillor and I would buy a quarter's worth of balls and try for a coconut. Then we'd come back and talk about next week's budget, which was still running at a hundred and thirty-two thousand dollars a day."

It wasn't until some time later that Allday was in a position to ask Saltzman what had gone on in New York.

"Everything's all right," Saltzman said.

Allday: "What do you mean by all right, Harry? Did they like the film?

Saltzman: "Of course they liked the film! What makes you think they didn't like the film?"

Allday: "Well, nobody said anything."

Saltzman: "Why did they have to say anything? If they'd hated the film that's when they would have said so. They liked it, so what did they need to say?"

Allday: "Well, it's a point of view."

Someone came up with a bunch of flowers for Mrs. Saltzman and there was a pause while they posed for a photograph. Then Allday said:

"You mean they really like it?"

Saltzman: "Of course they really like it! Would I say they did if they didn't?"

Allday: "No, Harry. But did they like it in—well, in

tangible terms? I mean, what about Check Day next Thursday? Do we have the money to pay?

Saltzman: "What was the budget when I left here yesterday?"

Allday: "Ten million dollars—and we're overspent."

Saltzman: "It is now thirteen million dollars. They gave me an extra three million. But that's the last. After that we're on our own. Do you think we can bring it in?"

They stood there, amid the raucous music of the hurdy-gurdies and the deep beat of a portable discotheque, eyeing each other. Finally, Allday said:

"There's one thing, Harry. Why don't you let Guy know that they liked it?"

Saltzman: "I did that yesterday. Sent him a cable."

As it Was in 1940

But if Adolf Hitler thought the hour of destiny was at hand, and if Herman Göring thought he had the RAF on the run, on September 14, 1940, they knew differently the following day.

September 15 was a day to remember.

From midmorning until evening, the German bombers and their escorting fighters came over in continuous waves.

Keith Park sent up twenty-three squadrons of his fighters to meet and harry them on their inward journey. To the north, Leigh-Mallory had his Big Wings waiting to get in among them.

They cut the German bomber formations to pieces. The Luftwaffe pilots, overwhelmed by the reckless bravery and aggressiveness of the incoming Spitfires, scattered and began unloading their bombs indiscriminately. They poured down upon London. But so did the bombers themselves, as the RAF fighters swooped in and opened fire. Bombs fell in Westminster, Lambeth, Lewisham, Camberwell, Bermondsey, Clapham, Tooting and Kensington. One bomber's wing crashed outside a Pimlico pub and was toasted by the delighted customers. A Dornier bomber smashed down in the yard of Victoria Station.

That night the BBC announced that 185 German

aircraft had been shot down in the course of the day's operations. The nation and the world saluted the fighter pilots of the Royal Air Force.

In fact, the figure of 185 was a gross exaggeration. When records were more closely examined, it was discovered that only 60 planes had been shot down. But dozens more had crashed on their way home and piled up on the beach at Cape Gris-Nez.

And in view of the steady losses which they had suffered over the past weeks, a loss of 60 aircraft was a serious blow to the Germans. For Hitler the day was a jolting disappointment. This was to be the day when he dealt the RAF a mortal blow—and then invaded.

Instead, it was the Luftwaffe which had been badly wounded. Angrily, the German führer called in Göring and there was a rancorous postmortem on the day's disasters.

Next day, Göring changed his tactics. Henceforth there would be no more daylight raids on London. His bombers would steal in by night.

As for Hitler, he took a bitter decision. He told his commanders to cancel plans for the invasion of Britain.

XIV
Fade-out

IN LATE SEPTEMBER 1968, I came back to England
again and drove out to Duxford airfield. If the
weather had been poor during the summer, it could
not compare with its atrociousness now that autumn
was here. The sky was a curdle of thunderclouds racing before the wind, and sheets of rain swept across
the landing field. The great hangar which had gone
up so gloriously in flame and smoke a few weeks ago
was now a wet, black, sodden pile of rubbage.

The atmosphere was grim, but purposeful. The air
unit was flying on borrowed time now, and everyone
knew it. The unit had been cut down to the bone. No
kind of weather conditions now were allowed to in-
terfere with the flying. They simply took off and
found some of the less turbulent air, and then the B-25
and the twin-seater camera planes started shooting.
Guy Hamilton was filling in the blank spaces.

"It's not pleasant flying in this muck," said John
Hawke, down for a quick drink between his first and
second sortie of the day, "but it's certainly a salutary

experience. The slackness has gone in this unit. We're getting the material—and it looks as exciting on the screen as it does when we take it."

"I never imagined that a landlubber like Hamilton would ever be able to stand it in this weather," said Ginger Lacey. "It can get pretty rough up there. The first time he went up he was ill, and the second time too, and I don't think it will be the last. It doesn't stop him from getting what he wants, though."

Guy Hamilton said: "Rough indeed! I wonder what all the people living along the east coast are going to think when they find all those little brown bags lying around in their gardens?"

He added: "One of the troubles with this unit was that they'd got slack. The pilots have been going on too long. A lot of the shots they got were good, but they weren't coordinated. Bits of bits and pieces. I'm here to get the dramatic bits that will sew them together. But the pilots are tired. They've been at it a long time—longer than the real Battle of Britain, in fact. Some of the planes have been getting ropey. Some of the Spanish pilots' contracts have been coming to an end. Why should they take any risks?"

So he had called them together for a conference, Spanish and British pilots together, and he had taken a calculated risk.

"I called them a bunch of old women," he said. "I told them they'd lost their daring and their skill, that they were frightened of coming in close to the camera plane, that they were worrying too much about their wives and children. It worked, too. They stamped out to their planes, determined to show me. They've been showing me ever since."

John Hawke had been listening, and afterwards he said:

"And do you know what he does if they still don't come close enough? He orders them to fly across our bows, and then he orders me to speed up until we shave the whiskers off their nostrils. It ain't safe nowadays, but it's much more exciting."

Johnny Jordan, the one-legged cameraman, limped into the mess. He had been dicing with death himself all morning. He had thought out a new way of making the parachute sequence in the film more exciting. He dangled by a parachute line below his helicopter to show what it was like for a pilot to be caught in his own fuselage; and then, still hanging in midair, he shot other planes and parachutists coming past him.

Guy Hamilton was very grateful to him. He was insisting that Jordan should be bought a special sheepskin jacket to keep out the cold as he twirled two thousand feet up over the battered cornfields of Cambridgeshire.

And so it was that at Duxford, in the cold sleet of September 1968, I watched the last shots being taken for *The Battle of Britain*.

One lunchtime, while everyone else was in the bar or the canteen, I wandered across the tarmac toward the line of Spitfires and Messerschmitts parked in the rain. It was a wicked day and everything in sight looked shoddy and sodden, except for the planes.

It was impossible to look at them without feeling sentimental. All summer long they had flown together in spite of the weather, the schedules and the bankers. We would never see their like gathered together like this again. With the ending of this film, they no longer had any raison d'être.

But at least, while *The Battle of Britain* was shooting, they had more than earned their keep; and thanks to the Spanish and Texan pilots who had ridden them so gallantly, the Messerschmitts had wiped the stain from the swastikas which they wore on their sides.

They made a brave sight in the rain, and I touched my forelock to them. No, we would never see their like again. Nor, I suspected, a film like *The Battle of Britain* either.

As It Was in 1940

There was to be another month of heavy raids on London, and there would be more air battles between British and German fighters over the Channel, but it can be definitely said that on September 15, 1940, the Battle of Britain was won.

Never again did the Germans ever hope to wipe out the RAF. Never again did Adolf Hitler believe in an invasion of Britain.

The battle had seen deeds of extraordinary skill and bravery by fighter pilots on both sides, and their names were soon to become a legend: "Sailor" Malan, Douglas Bader, "Ginger" Lacey, Stanford-Tuck, Al Deere, Adolf Galland, Werner Mölders.

They flew on and they survived.

But for Sir Hugh Dowding, the man who had controlled the battle, whose coolness and perspicacity had helped to meet Göring's challenge and exploit his mistakes, the outcome was less happy. He was quietly retired and fobbed off with a title. He had fought and won the most vital air engagement of World War II, but he was the only successful commander in control of a major air battle who, when that war ended, was not made a marshal of the Royal Air Force.

Air Chief Marshal Sir Sholto Douglas took over as the commanding officer of Fighter Command. Leigh-

Mallory was given command of Keith Park's 11 Group, the group which had so splendidly and successfully borne the brunt of the battle. Keith Park was moved out to a training command.

And only now, in 1969, is Lord Dowding emerging from the shadows and from behind the intriguers to get the credit that is his undoubted due.

GROUP #2 IN THIS HIGHLY PRAISED
SERIES . . .

BALLANTINE'S ILLUSTRATED HISTORY OF WORLD WAR II

Four new titles have now been added to this important new
series of all-original BIG SIZE war histories—each book measur-
ing 8¼" by 5½" and profusely illustrated with approximately
150 rare photographs, combat maps and detailed drawings:

STALINGRAD: the turning point,
by Geoffrey Jukes

AIRCRAFT CARRIER: the majestic weapon,
by Captain Donald Macintyre

BASTOGNE: the road block,
by Peter Elstob

PANZER DIVISION: the mailed fist,
by Major K. J. Macksey

"An auspicious start . . . Emphasis is on photographs, some of
rare vintage, yet the text in each case is solid and authoritative,
written with spirit. Readers who continue to be fascinated by
the manifold aspects of World War II, the largest single event in
the 20th Century, will find these books a bargain, not only because of their price but also their contents."

—Martin Blumenson, former Chief Historian,
U. S. Office of Military History

Each book is priced at $1.00—or you can order all four books
delivered postage free to your home by sending $4.00 to

BALLANTINE BOOKS, 36 WEST 20TH STREET, NEW YORK, N.Y.
10003